10 Minute Torah Talks

Weekly Parsha Insights

By

Rabbi Joseph Bronner

DEDICATION

This book is lovingly dedicated to my family past, present and future:

My parents ~ Shlomo Aryeh and Channah Bronner, ז"צל,

my parents-in-law ~ Rabbi Yitzchok and
Rebbetzin Rachel Amsel, ז"צל,

my wife ~ Dr. Leila Leah Bronner,
without whom this book would never have seen the light of day.

My children and children-in-law ~
Temi & Dr. Bernie Monderer,
Moshe & Amira Bronner,
Esthie & Walter Feinblum,

my grandchildren and great-grandchildren.

עֲטֶרֶת זְקֵנִים בְּנֵי בָנִים וְתִפְאֶרֶת בָּנִים אֲבוֹתָם.

Grandchildren are the pride and joy of old age and children take
great pride in their parents (Mishlei 17:6).

CONTENTS

i

INTRODUCTION

This book represents the culmination of a long and fruitful career in which learning Torah was, thankfully, a focus and a guide. Throughout my life I have endeavored, in a small way, to promote Jewish life and to inculcate a love of Torah in Jewish people, young and old. In that spirit, I would like to pass on some of the insights that I have had the honor of learning, particularly as they relate to Jewish life today. I hope that these words on the weekly parshiyos will be enlightening, both for my own family and for Jewish readers everywhere, so that they might know more about our great and profound heritage.

I was born in Berlin to Hasidic-minded parents from Poland. As the Nazis rose to power we fled Germany for Belgium, where I studied in a yeshivah in Heide, 20 minutes by train from Antwerp. That small yeshivah of 100 boys, though materially lacking (without even running water), was a spiritual powerhouse where I developed a palpable passion for Gemara that impacted me forever. On Friday, May 10, 1940, Germany invaded Belgium and Antwerp was no longer a safe haven. With seven of us packed into a car like sardines, we traveled to Bordeaux, in southern France. Inexplicably, we were able to cross the bridge to safety in Spain, but we were the last; the bridge was closed immediately afterwards, preventing other refugees from escaping Nazi hands. In short, we managed, with great pain and difficulty, but thanks to many chasdei HaShem (near miracles) to reach Lisbon. From there we continued to the United States.

In New York, I studied in the Beis Hamidrash of Yeshivas Chaim Berlin and received semichah from HaRav HaGaon Yitzchok Hutner זצ"ל. Then my father, ע"ה, sent my wife and me to South Africa, baby daughter in tow. There, while I managed a diamond business connected to De Beers, Rabbi Dr. Michael Kosowsky זצ"ל, who was a leading rabbi in South Africa, had me take over the teaching of four boys from the Bnei Akiva youth movement. This small group was enlarged after some time and, b'ezras

HaShem, Rabbi Kosowsky and I founded Yeshiva College, the very first yeshivah in South Africa, which prospers even today in the 21st century. It was and continues to be affiliated with Mizrachi South Africa, which I represented at the Zionist Federation of South Africa for 15 years.

In the 1980s we returned to America, settling in Los Angeles. There, together with other dedicated families, we became involved with Kehillas Yavneh and its expansion. That exceptional community, with its own excellent yeshivah, flourishes today.

This book is compiled from a selection of my divrei Torah delivered over the years on Shabbos afternoons during shalosh seudos at Yavneh in Los Angeles. Its contents may be rewardingly employed at the Shabbos table, at a bar mitzvah or a wedding, and perhaps even at your own shalosh seudos. These 10-minute talks may not be earth-shattering, but they present the essence of each parashah with reference mainly to the Rishonim. In particular, they relate the parashah to current events today, both globally and in ארץ ישראל. The world changes, but the Torah does not. For that simple reason, we read and re-read the parshiyos, year in and year out, noting that even the great commentators over the centuries held divergent views and on whose giant shoulders we gratefully stand.

These talks are a legacy that I hope my children will embrace; a kind of ethical will. They are bound up with a confirmation that we live in the beginning of ימות המשיח, the Messianic Age, otherwise known as אתחלתא דגאולה, the beginning of redemption.

Note:
In order to present the Torah with fidelity, the text contains both Hebrew and English.
In general, the transliteration follows the principles of Artscroll, employing "Ashkenazi" consonants and "Sefardi" vowels. Names are generally found in Hebrew transliteration: Moshe, not Moses.

10 Minute Torah Talks
Weekly Parsha Insights

Rabbi Joseph Bronner

1 SEFER BEREISHIS

Parashas Bereishis

The first three prakim of Bereishis tell us of the creation of the world, the creation of man, Adam's sin and, finally, Adam's expulsion from גן עדן (the Garden of Eden). In these prakim, events of normal, natural life, as well as supernatural occurrences, are related. This essay attempts to understand Adam's sin, as well as the nature of the Tree of Knowledge of Good and Evil and the characteristics of גן עדן itself.

"HaShem caused to sprout from the ground every tree that was pleasing to the sight and good for food, ועץ החיים בתוך הגן ועץ הדעת טוב ורע, and the Tree of Life in the midst of the garden and the Tree of Knowledge of Good and Evil" (Bereishis 2:9). HaShem tested Adam by saying to him, "מכל עץ הגן אכל תאכל, "Of every tree in the garden you may freely eat," ומעץ הדעת טוב ורע לא תאכל ממנו, "but of the Tree of Knowledge of Good and Bad you must not eat thereof," כי ביום אכלך ממנו מות תמות, "for on the day you eat of it, you shall surely die" (Bereishis 2:16-17).

The רבונו של עולם, the Creator of the world and of man, is also the Creator of moral values. This reality was confirmed and emphasized by the serpent, who enticed Chavah by saying, "On the day you eat of [the Tree of Knowledge], your eyes will be opened והייתם כאלקים ידעי טוב ורע, and you will be like G-d, knowing good and bad" (Bereishis 3:5). So the sin of Adam was that he aspired to steal from HaShem the ability to determine the criteria for his own moral judgment. Eating from the Tree of Knowledge meant that Adam had acquired the power of HaShem to differentiate between good and evil.

My father-in-law, Rav Yitzchak Amsel זצ"ל, was a great mekubal. He taught that the *Zohar* interprets this sin as an act of rebellion against HaShem. It is similar to the rebellion found in the story of the 12 spies (Bamidbar 13). HaShem had repeatedly declared that כנען, Canaan, was a "good land," but 10 of the spies brought back an evil report, saying, "It is a land that devours its inhabitants" (Bamidbar 13:32). So great was this sin that it was not until that generation – the slave generation of the Exodus – had died out and a new generation had taken its place that Israel was deemed worthy to inherit the Holy Land.

Must we assume that the Tree of Knowledge, the fruit of which would endow Adam with the capacity to distinguish between good and evil, was somehow extraordinary? Would the fruit of the Tree of Knowledge suddenly bestow upon Adam a clear comprehension of moral values? If so, why should that knowledge have been forbidden to him under penalty of death?

Rabbi Samson Raphael Hirsch (1808-1888), inspired by the 12th century Rambam's commentary on Mishnah Sanhedrin (10:1), believed that the Garden is an actual place in this world and that the Tree of Knowledge of Good and Evil was, superficially, exactly like every other tree in גן עדן. Yet, it differed from the other trees in that it could reveal to Adam a fundamental doctrine: That good and evil are determined by HaShem. Adam was made to realize that human reasoning cannot be the arbiter in determining moral values.

However, most Rishonim did not think that גן עדן is an actual place in this world. About 100 years after the Rambam, the great halachist and mystic, the 13th century Ramban (1194-1270) declared in *Sefer Sha'ar HaGamul* that גן עדן is עולם הנשמות, the world of the souls; in other words, a purely spiritual domain. This is the view that has prevailed among בני ישראל, as illustrated by the invocation of גן עדן in the memorial prayer קל מלא רחמים, in which we say, in reference to the souls of the departed, בגן עדן תהא מנוחתם , "may their resting place be in the Garden of Eden." It is noteworthy that Rabbi Samson Raphael Hirsch, perhaps because of his rationalist leanings, did not include קל מלא רחמים in his siddur.

These two ways of looking at גן עדן result from the fact that the spiritual and physical functioned together in the Garden. As long as they were in גן עדן the snake could speak and the tree could impart spiritual knowledge.

Mishnah Tamid (7:4), which we read after אין כאלקינו in Shabbos Musaf, explains how the physical and spiritual join together. The subject of this Mishnah is the שיר של יום, the daily prayers that the Leviim sang during services in the Beis Hamikdash, and the Mishnah teaches us which prayer was said on each day. With regard to מזמור שיר ליום השבת, the "Psalm for Shabbos," the Mishnah explains that מזמור שיר לעתיד לבוא, "it is a psalm, a song for the future to come, for the day that will be entirely Shabbos and contentment for eternal life." So, not only גן עדן but Shabbos, too, combines the natural and the super-natural.

The *Zohar* takes this idea one step further. In its discussion of Parashas Yisro, it says, "Come and see, in the six days of the week, when Minchah arrives, harsh judgments rule and every harsh judgment is awakened. But on Shabbos, when Minchah comes, it is a time of רעוא דרעוין, when HaShem's deepest favors are to be found; the favors of HaShem come forth and all harshness disappears." And therefore, שלוש סעודות, the third meal on Shabbos, marks the pinnacle of the spirituality of Shabbos. It is the realization of עולם הבא, the World to Come, in עולם הזה, this world. It is a moment when the physical and the spiritual intermingle. In other words, it is מעין עולם הבא; it is the taste of גן עדן.

Parashas Noach

Parashas Noach tells us of two generations – or rather, two civilizations – that flourished, but in the end failed as a result of their sins. One civilization is referred to as דור המבול, the Generation of the Flood, the other as דור הפלגה, the Generation of the Dispersion, or the builders of the Tower of Bavel. Both were uniquely punished for their own, separate sins.

Rashi (11th century), in his commentary on Bereishis 11:9, asks, "Which sin was graver: That of the Generation of the Flood, or that of those who built the Tower of Bavel? The former, the people of the flood generation, did not raise up their hands against HaShem, whereas the latter, the people of the tower, raised up their hands in open revolt. Yet the former generation was drowned, while the latter did not perish." Rashi goes on to explain that the people of the flood robbed and fought each other, and hence perished; while the people of the tower, although they raised their hands against HaShem, lived together in harmony and relative friendship. Rashi states that the mitzvos between man and his fellow man are paramount and can never be absolved by HaShem if they have not been forgiven by the person who was wronged; while the mitzvos between man and HaShem are forgiven by HaShem after a person does teshuvah. This is a universal principle and is applicable not only to the Jewish people but to all inhabitants of the world. Therefore, the Generation of the Flood was utterly destroyed while the Generation of the Dispersion would ultimately survive.

The Midrash tells us that the Generation of the Dispersion built their tower very high as a sign of their domination of the world. In claiming dominion over all the people of the world, they aspired to challenge HaShem. In response to their actions, HaShem decided to punish the Generation of the Dispersion by sending them from their homeland and dispersing them throughout the world. Furthermore, said HaShem to the angels,

"Let us descend and there confuse their language, that they should not understand one another's speech" (Bereishis 11:7).

We are reminded of what the Ramban said about HaShem's instruction to Adam and Chavah after their creation, ומלאו את הארץ וכבשוה, "Fill the earth and subdue it" (Bereishis 1:28). The Ramban writes that HaShem gave them power and dominion over the earth to do as they wished with the cattle, the reptiles and that which crawled on the ground and, in addition, to pluck up that which He planted, and to dig copper and other ores from the hills. Essentially, the Ramban declares here that the Torah gives man the right to take all natural resources from the earth for his absolute benefit, in order to create and develop a world in which he would live more securely and safely. In other words, to make the world a better place for all mankind.

Furthermore, when we, the Jewish people, recite Kiddush on Friday night, we start with the words, ויכלו השמים והארץ, "Heaven and Earth were finished" (Bereishis 2:1), a passage that concludes, "and He sanctified [the Seventh Day] because on it, He abstained from all His work אשר ברא אלקים לעשות, which HaShem created to make" (Bereishis 2:3). The difficulty in this verse is the meaning of לעשות, "to make." HaShem just created (ברא) the world; what else has to be done? The Midrash explains that HaShem created an imperfect world; man is called upon to improve and perfect the world to make it a better and safer place to live.

Similarly, Midrash Tanchuma on Parashas Tazria relates the famous story of the Roman governor's challenge to Rabbi Akiva about the mitzvah of circumcision. The governor challenged him, "Isn't HaShem's creation better than man's?" In response, Rabbi Akiva brought raw wheat in one hand, and man-made bread in the other, and then flax in one hand, and cloth in the other. In this way, he showed man's partnership with HaShem in perfecting the world. This is the meaning of לעשות; humanity must become a partner with HaShem in creation.

While HaShem gave human beings the ability to use technology to improve their lives, as technological advances have accelerated in the modern age they have often been put to use by man in destructive and morally questionable ways. When man makes progress in the material aspect of civilization, he must not forget that the spiritual and moral values that HaShem bestowed upon mankind must remain the bedrock of civilization. The Generation of the Dispersion rejected HaShem and embraced the physical and mundane achievements of human effort; they thereby created a world devoid of moral values.

Avraham Avinu, who lived at the time of the tower and witnessed it, came to believe in HaShem and to serve Him (Rambam, *Mishneh Torah*, Hilchot Avodas Kochavim v'Chokoseihem, 1:3). Then he showed his neighbors that avodah zarah is the greatest sin. The Rambam writes, "Thousands and tens of thousands gathered around Avraham עד שיחזירהו לדרך האמת, until they returned to the path of truth." This path of truth leads away from incorrect belief and incorrect behavior. The Rambam continues, "Rejection of idolatry is [the prerequisite for] acceptance of the Torah; it is the basis for all the mitzvos." (2:4) By bringing the people of his generation to accept ethical monotheism – the opposite of the Generation of the Flood, and belief in HaShem – the opposite of the Generation of the Tower, Avraham Avinu taught us how to lay the foundation for a just and prosperous civilization.

Parashas Lech Lecha

Parashas Lech Lecha opens with the words, "HaShem said to Avram, 'Go for yourself from your land, from your relatives and from your father's house, to the land that I will show you. And I will make you a great nation, and I will bless you... and all the families of the earth shall be blessed by you'" (Bereishis 12:1-3). However, the Torah does not tell us why Avram – as he was known before his bris milah (Bereishis 17:5) – was chosen.

The Rambam's *Mishneh Torah* is a halachic work but, extraordinarily, the Rambam dedicates the first perek of Hilchos Avodah Zarah to the life of Avraham, whom he calls the עמודו של עולם, the pillar of the whole world. He describes Avraham's great faith in HaShem, his righteousness and his love for humankind. Rambam stresses Avraham's realization that one invisible and merciful G-d created the world and mankind. For this reason, he risked his life to teach monotheism to idol worshippers.

However, the Maharal of Prague (16th century), in his famous work *נצח ישראל*, *The Eternity of Israel*, offers a totally different explanation of HaShem's choice of Avraham. In chapter 11, he declares that HaShem chose Avraham, not because of his personal greatness – and he was great – but in order to father the nation that would become a גוי קדוש, "a holy nation." Avraham served only as a means to a greater end. The nation to be established, עם ישראל, was to become the instrument of HaShem's purpose.

Faced with the differing views of the Rambam and the Maharal, we must ask: Is Avraham the father of only the Jewish people or is he also the father of all of mankind, in the sense that he brought ethical monotheism into the world? The beginning of this parashah gives us an indication. The three opening psukim, which contain HaShem's first revelation to Avraham, show HaShem's absolute separation of Avraham from the rest of mankind. Avraham is asked to leave his father's house and his family, his birthplace and the nation in which he grew up.

However, the following psukim show precisely the opposite, Avraham's future universalism, which includes all of mankind, by revealing HaShem's promise: ונברכו בך כל משפחת האדמה, "and all the families of the earth shall be blessed by you" (Bereishis 12:3). Not only would Avraham become the father of the people of Israel, but he would also be a blessing for all nations.

The immense responsibility of Avraham's charge is revealed throughout the chapters of the parashah. Avraham's first covenant with HaShem is the ברית בין הבתרים, "the covenant between the pieces" (Bereishis 15:7-21). HaShem directs Avraham to prepare a number of specified animals to be cut in half; as well as a turtledove and a pigeon, which were not cut in half because the pigeon is the symbol of the Jewish people. The ceremony of the covenant required that the two parties pass between the separated halves of the animals. As Joseph Albo (Spain, 15th century) pointed out, just as the two parts of each animal had formed one body, each feeling the pain of the other, so the two parties making the covenant were to be as one body forever. As a symbol of the covenant, a flaming torch symbolizing HaShem passed between the pieces. In the psukim that follow, we read, "On that day, HaShem made a covenant with Avraham, saying, 'To your descendants have I given this Land, from the river of Egypt to the great river, the Euphrates River'" (Bereishis 15:18). The ברית בין הבתרים is an eternal covenant between HaShem and Avraham but, most importantly, HaShem extends it to his descendents, the Children of Israel, for all future generations.

Chapter 14 reveals that Avraham was both vital for the creation of the Jewish people and also concerned about the welfare of the nations of his time. The Torah tells us that Avraham supported the five kings against the four kings and participated in battles for their benefit (Bereishis 14). Yet, the five nations with which Avraham allied himself are mentioned at the end of the ברית בין הבתרים and later become the territory of ארץ ישראל. The same nations are also listed at the end of the book of Bamidbar and at the beginning of the book of Devarim, before בני ישראל conquer the Promised Land. Their identification indicates the fulfillment of HaShem's covenant with Avraham. Avraham's participation in the battles suggests that Avraham symbolically took title to the Holy Land before his descendants actually inhabited the Land.

Later in the parashah, HaShem gives Avram the new name of Avraham (Bereishis 17). At that time, HaShem says, "As for Me, this is My covenant with you: You shall be אב המון גוים, a father to a multitude of nations" (Bereishis 17:4). Rashi comments that the new name, אברהם, is an acrostic. Originally, his name was אברם, the father of Aram, which points to his individuality. Rashi remarks that his new name should have been אבהם, an acronym based on אב המון גוים. However, HaShem wanted Avraham to bear a name expressing both his identity as the universal father of all nations and, at the same time, the national father of נצח ישראל, the eternal people.

In conclusion, it is clear, as indicated in the opening psukim of the parashah, that Avraham is a universal father, as pointed out by the Rambam and, at the same time, the father of the chosen and eternal nation of Israel, as taught by the Maharal.

Parashas Vayera

עקידת יצחק, the Binding of Yitzchak, is certainly one of the most challenging acts of faith recorded in the Torah. We will discuss the views of the Rishonim of the 12th and 13th centuries, who differ significantly in their understanding of עקידת יצחק.

The Rambam, in his *Moreh Nevuchim, Guide to the Perplexed* (3:24), offers the traditional explanation of עקידת יצחק. The opening verse of the account reads, "And it happened after these things that HaShem tested Avraham" (Bereishis 22:1). The Rambam makes it very clear that HaShem is not testing Avraham because He wants to discover something that is doubtful in His mind. On the contrary, HaShem is omniscient, all-knowing. Rather, the "test" is a trial for Avraham, intended to serve as an attestation to the world that man can raise himself above his selfishness and move toward values that transcend the material world. Avraham was sterile and childless when HaShem promised him that he would father a great nation. Finally, in his old age, a son was born to him. Then came the call for the binding of Yitzchak. Avraham knew only loyalty to HaShem and submission to His will. He was possessed by אהבת ה' ויראת ה' – love of HaShem and fear of HaShem. He did not challenge HaShem's demand, but reacted with willingness to offer his most precious son on the altar he had prepared.

The Ramban extends the Rambam's interpretation that "Avraham was tested by HaShem," introducing the idea that the test was not adminstered to Avraham for the benefit of the tester but rather for the benefit of the tested, לטובת המנוסה. By testing Avraham, HaShem gave him an opportunity to bring a good deed "from potential into actuality, so that he may be rewarded for a good deed, not for a good thought alone" (Bereishis 22:1).

The Rambam makes a second insightful and original observation regarding Avraham's trial. The Binding of Yitzchak demonstrates the absolute validity of prophetic truth. The נביא, the prophet, is as certain of his prophecy as he is of any factual knowledge. Had

Avraham harbored even the slightest doubt that he may have fallen victim to misapprehension or hallucination, he could not have been ready to sacrifice his son. According to the Rambam, this absolute clarity characterizes all prophets of Israel. Thus, the brachah said before the reading of the haftarah refers to נביאים טובים, "good prophets," whose words are נאמרים באמת, "uttered with truth." The prophets themselves are thus distinguished by being נביאי האמת וצדק, "the prophets of truth and righteousness."

The Rambam, in his *Mishneh Torah* on the laws of idol worship, states that Avraham had the greatest emunah in HaShem of any person in the Torah. As an expression of this emunah, he bound his son Yitzchak on the altar. Yet, at the same time, Avraham had emunah in the ברית בין הבתרים, the covenant in which HaShem declares, לזרעך נתתי את הארץ הזאת, "to your descendents have I given this Land" (Bereishis 15:18). The Binding of Yitzchak looked like it would cancel that covenant because there would be no offspring to whom to give the Land. Yet, the עקידה ends with the call of the angel: "Avraham, Avraham, do not stretch out your hand against the lad or do anything against him" (Bereishis 22:12), confirming Avraham's faith that HaShem would find a way to reconcile the עקידה with the ברית בין הבתרים.

The Rashbam, the grandson of Rashi, explains עקידת יצחק from a different point of view. He understands the episode to be punishing Avraham for his lack of emunah in HaShem. The Rashbam explains that עקידת יצחק starts with the words, "And it happened after these things" (Bereishis 22:1). This introductory phrase connects the עקידה with events related earlier in the parashah. The peace treaty Avraham made with Avimelech, the king of Gerar, yielded to him a portion of the Holy Land: Gerar, the land inhabited by the Philistines, known today as the Gaza Strip. The text tells us that Avimelech said to Avraham, " 'Now swear to me here by HaShem that you will not deal falsely with me, nor with my child nor with my grandchild; according to the kindness that I have done with you, do with me, and with the land in which you have sojourned.' And Avraham said, 'I will swear' " (Bereishis 21:23-24).

Avimelech brazenly demonstrated his cynical character. Where was the חסד he claimed to have shown to Avraham? He had kidnapped Sarah (Bereishis 20:2) and, only under severe warning from HaShem, returned her the next day. He had then claimed that allowing Avraham to live in Beer Sheva was an act of חסד, as if Beer Sheva were part of the land of the Philistines. Yet "the two of them entered into a covenant" (Bereishis 21:27).

According to the Rashbam's understanding, HaShem was angry that Avraham had so little emunah as to cede a part of ארץ ישראל. Therefore, HaShem punished Avraham by asking him to sacrifice his son Yitzchak, saying: "We will then see, when you are without Yitzchak, how you will be able to keep for generations your covenant with Avimelech!" עקידת יצחק was not a testing of Avraham's faith, as the Rambam holds, but a punishment for his lack of faith.

In conclusion, history has shown that the Rashbam is correct in pointing out HaShem's great displeasure at Avraham's ceding of Gerar – the Gaza Strip. Rashbam's understanding has even greater ramifications today. We believe that under no circumstances can we cede any part of the Holy Land to the enemies of Israel; and certainly not when the Jewish people are dwelling on the Land.

Parashas Chayei Sarah

In לך לך, the parashah read two weeks ago, the Torah records the ברית בין הבתרים, "the covenant between the pieces" (Bereishis 15:9-21), in which HaShem promised Avraham the Holy Land for the nation that he would father. In this week's parshah, חיי שרה, Avraham begins to make HaShem's promise a reality by buying מערת המכפלה, the Cave of Machpelah in חברון, Chevron, in order to bury Sarah, who had died suddenly, immediately after עקידת יצחק. Why did Avraham insist on buying מערת המכפלה, spurning all other options?

The Hittites offered Avraham the choicest of their burial places, free of any payment (Bereishis 23:6). Avraham rejected their kind offer, asking them to intercede with Ephron to "grant me the Cave of Machpelah which is his, on the edge of his field; let him grant it to me for its full price as an estate for a burial site" (Bereishis 23:9). Why was only מערת המכפלה suitable as an eternal resting place for Sarah, the mother of Israel? Because this was the site where, tradition held, Adam and Chavah were buried.

All human beings are the physical descendants of Adam and Chavah, but only Avraham and Sarah are their spiritual descendants. Sarah was Chavah's spiritual successor, her spiritual continuation. It is for this reason that Avraham was intent on burying Sarah next to Chavah, whose beliefs and ideology she cherished. Sarah's mission was the continuation of Chavah's, whom Adam had named אם כל חי, "mother of all the living" (Bereishis 3:20). Sarah had at first been named Sarai, "my princess," but HaShem changed her name to Sarah because, as Rashi comments, שתהא שרה על כל העולם כולו, "She is to be the princess of the whole world" (Rashi on Bereishis 17:15). She now became a universal figure, bearing an appellation similar to that of Chavah, her spiritual ancestress.

Sarah not only continued the mission entrusted to Chavah, but surpassed her. Chavah had failed by misleading Adam and thereby bringing death upon the world. Sarah taught the women belief in HaShem and thereby brought blessings upon the world (Rashi on Bereishis 12:5). When Avraham hesitated to send Hagar and Ishmael away upon the urging of Sarah, HaShem confirmed the spiritual greatness of Sarah by advising Avraham, "Whatever Sarah tells you, heed her voice" (Bereishis 21:12).

Let us now turn to Avraham, who would also be buried in מערת המכפלה. In our tradition, Avraham continues to fulfill the purpose for which Adam was created. Pirkei Avos expresses this idea by stating, "There are 10 generations from Noach to Avraham, to make known the patience of HaShem, for all those generations continued provoking Him until Avraham Avinu came and received the reward they should all have earned" (Avos 5:3). Avraham is thus the תכלית, the purpose of Creation, as we read in Parashas Bereishis, אלה תולדות השמים והארץ בהבראם, "These are the products of the heaven and the earth when they were created" (Bereishis 2:4). The Midrash interprets this verse homiletically, declaring, "Do not read בהבראם, but rearrange the letters, and read באברהם." This commentary suggests that the world was created for Avraham's appearance, at some future time, as the impetus for a new start for humanity.

In a similar vein, the Jewish people, like Avraham, are called upon to spiritually elevate mankind. Because the Jewish people are the only ones to whom HaShem gave the Torah, His blueprint for existence, only they are endowed with the spiritual capacity to elevate mankind to live witout sin. This is a concept developed by Rav Moshe Hayim Luzzatto (1707-1746) in his book דרך השם, The Way of HaShem. Such a world, he writes, will fulfil the prophecy of the prophet Yoel: "And it will happen after this that I shall pour out My spirit upon all flesh" (Yoel 3:1). Similarly, of the Messianic Age, Yeshayahu prophesied: "They will neither injure nor destroy in all of my sacred mountain; for the earth will be filled with knowledge of HaShem as the water covering the sea bed" (Yeshayahu 2:9). By invoking the uneven sea bed with its underwater mountains and deep troughs and comparing it to the even surface of the sea, Yeshayahu indicates that all people, whatever their personal traits, will one day share equally the belief in the One G-d who created the universe and all it contains. Such a circumstance, at the end of days, will be the realization of the efforts of the Children of Israel, the spiritual and physical heirs of Avraham and Sarah.

There are spiritual encounters between this world and those who are no longer with us. A person's grave – the site of his final presence in the physical world – maintains a thin bond with the deceased, a slight closeness with his soul and his spirit. The Gemara in Berachos 18b relates the visitation of spirits to the site of their mortal remains. It is for this reason that we visit the graves of our father and mother, speaking to them and praying for their blessings. For the same reason, it is a mitzvah להשתטח על קברי צדיקים, to pray at the tombs of the tzaddikim, including Avraham and Sarah, with faith that they will intercede on our behalf for חיים טובים, a healthy and happy life.

Parashas Toldos

Parashas Toldos describes the bestowal of ברכת אברהם, the ancestral blessings of Avraham, on Yaakov, the younger son of Yitzchak and Rivkah, rather than on Esav, his very slightly older twin brother. Sefer Bereishis expresses itself in narrative form and, after reading its surface meaning, we turn to the נביאים and חז"ל to interpret and judge the events in the story.

At first, we might wonder whether Yaakov was the right recipient of the ברכה. After all, when Yitzchak asked Yaakov, מי אתה בני, "Who are you, my son?" Ya'akov answered, אנכי עשו בכרך, "I am Esav your first-born" (Bereishis 27:18-19). Furthermore, Yitzchak said to Esav, בא אחיך במירמה ויקח ברכתך, "your brother came with deceit and took your blessing" (Bereishis 27:35). Though Yitzchak said that Yaakov acted במירמה, with deceit, he adds, גם ברוך יהיה, "Indeed he shall remain blessed" (Bereishis 27:33). Can we find anywhere an explicit statement that Yaakov is a righteous and trustworthy personality?

The נביאים and later, חז"ל, demonstrate Yaakov's essential righteousness and confirm Yaakov as the proper recipient of the blessing. The prophet Michah pronounces a phrase that we recite in ובא לציון גואל twice every day in our prayers, תתן אמת ליעקב חסד לאברהם, "give the truth to Yaakov and kindness to Avraham" (Michah 7:20). Michah conveys to us HaShem's confirmation that just as Avraham is blessed with loving kindness, Yaakov is the embodiment of truth. Indeed, Yaakov is known as בחיר האבות, the "chosen among the Patriarchs." It is for this reason that the author of *Targum Onkolos* (1st century) renders the word, במירמה, "with deceit," in the pasuk we quoted above (Bereishis 27:35), using the word בחוכמתא, "with cleverness." Onkelos is not strictly translating, but rather takes on the role of a commentator, confirming the truthfulness and moral integrity of Yaakov Avinu. The sages of the Talmud followed this interpretation in their writings about Yaakov.

In the parashah, at the very end of chapter 26, we read that "when Esav was 40 years old, he took as his wife Judith, daughter of Beeri the Hittite, and Basmath, daughter of Elon the Hittite, and they were a source of spiritual rebellion to Yitzchak and Rivkah." (Bereishis 26:34-35) Here, the Torah confirms that Esav is unworthy to continue the patriarchal line of Avraham and Yitzchak because Esav intermarried with the Hittites, an act that Avraham had explicitly forbidden (Bereishis 24:3).

In his commentary on the parashah, Rashi goes even further, showing no hesitation in exposing the fundamental characters of Yaakov and Esav. Quoting the Gemara and the Midrash, he portrays the saga of the brothers, not as a family quarrel but rather as a cosmic struggle. According to Rashi, two brothers, two nations and two worlds are striving for domination. As HaShem declares, "two regimes shall be born from you, and the elder shall serve the younger" (Bereishis 25:23). Rashi, quoting the Midrash, says that this struggle was between עולם הזה and עולם הבא, between the material world and the spiritual world. Each brother sought to dominate both worlds.

According to Bereishis Rabba, when, during her pregnancy, Rivkah passed by the entrance to a beis midrash, Yaakov kicked to get out of her womb. Esav, on the other hand, kicked to get out when she passed by a place of idol worship. From this, Rashi concludes that Esav was an עובד עבודה זרה, an idol worshipper, while Yaakov was a true believer in HaShem. Rashi states his conclusions clearly and succinctly: Esav, as a servant of עבודה זרה, גילוי עריות ושפיכות דמים, idol worship, sexual transgression, and murder, is a רשע, while Yaakov is a צדיק. At stake in the struggle between them was no less a matter than who would rule over שני העולמות, the two worlds, and thus whether the spiritual world would prevail over the material world, or vice versa. Furthermore, according to tradition, Esav is the father of Edom, the symbol for Rome, Christian persecution and all of the enemies of the Jewish people.

Yitzchak may have said that Yaakov acted במירמה, with deceit when he received his father's blessing but, according to Rashi, when Yaakov bought the בכורה, the rights of the firstborn from Esav, Yaakov legitimately acquired the prerogatives and responsibilities of the firstborn and therefore received ברכת אברהם by right. Further on, we read, ויבז עשו את הבכורה, "Esav relinquished his birthright" (Bereishis 25:34). He did so with disdain because he did not wish to take on the obligations attached to being the firstborn. Yaakov and Rivkah understood the importance to future generations of the historic role that Yaakov had been by chosen by HaShem to fill. He was destined to become בחיר האבות, the chosen of the Patriarchs.

Parashas Vayeitzei

The parashah starts with the dream of Yaakov, in which he sees a ladder extending to Heaven with angels ascending and descending, and HaShem standing over him. Rashi, quoting the Midrash, comments that HaShem was present לשמרו, meaning "to watch and guard him."

The dream mentioned in the parashah, like all the dreams found in the books of the תנ"ך, is a vehicle of revelation. In the book of Bamidbar, when HaShem spoke to Aharon and Miriam, He specified, "If there shall be prophets among you, in a vision shall I, HaShem, make Myself known to him, in a dream shall I speak to him" (Bamidbar 12:6). The rabbinic comment concerning normal dreams – those not mentioned in the תנ"ך – suggests that חלום אחד משישים לנבואה, a dream can be considered to be up to one-sixtieth of prophesy (Berachos 57b).

My experience with dreams has made me believe firmly that dreams can contain messages about the future. When the German Blitzkrieg started on May 10, 1940, Belgium was quickly overrun, but my family escaped from Antwerp to France. We traveled by car. We were seven people, including five members of my family, and for six days we were just 10 kilometers ahead of the advancing Nazi army. My mother ע"ה often had dreams and intuitions and, during our flight from Belgium, she directed us in a way that allowed us to elude the enemy. It was due to her dreams and intuitions that we reached Bordeaux, and from there Spain and eventually neutral Portugal.

Our scholars have divided the dreams of Sefer Bereishis into two categories. The first comprises dreams in which HaShem actually speaks to the sleeping person. For example, HaShem tells Avimelech, King of Gerar, who had taken Sarah into his harem, "You are to die because of the woman you have taken" (Bereishis 20:3). Also, HaShem tells Lavan in a dream, "Beware, lest you speak with Yaakov either good or bad" (Bereishis 31:24).

In dreams of the second category, HaShem sends messages to the sleeping person, not by direct address but through imagery and movement, such as Joseph's vision of sheaves of wheat bowing down to him (Bereishis 37:7), and Pharaoh's dream of thin cows swallowing fat cows (Bereishis 41:4).

The dream of Yaakov on Mount Moriah fits into both of these categories. It contains a powerful pictoral message: The ladder to heaven with the angels ascending and descending. But HaShem also speaks directly to Yaakov; in fact, HaShem confers on him ברכת אברהם, the blessing of Avraham. He also blesses Yaakov, והנה אנוכי עמך, "Behold I am with you, I will guard you wherever you go and I will return you to this soil" (Bereishis 28:15). Yaakov is thus confirmed as the third forefather, after Avraham and Yitzchak. HaShem promises nationhood to his seed and ארץ ישראל as the homeland for the Eternal People.

Commenting on the dream, *Pirkei d'Rabbi Eliezer* explains, "Yaakov was shown the guardian angels of the Four Kingdoms that would ascend to dominate Israel. Yaakov saw each angel climbing a number of rungs corresponding to the years of its dominion and then descending as its reign ended. Babylon's angel climbed 70 rungs and then went down. Media's (Persia's) angel climbed 52 rungs and Greece's angel climbed 130. But the angel of Edom, which is Esav, kept climbing indefinitely, symbolizing the ascent of Rome and its many successors, even up to present times (the Nazis). Yaakov was frightened until HaShem assured him, והנה אנוכי עמך, and behold, I am with you (Bereishis 28:15).

Midrash Rabbah, however, regards the dream not as directed to Yaakov the individual but rather to Yaakov representing the entire Jewish people until the end of time. The Jews have witnessed the rise of mighty empires, including Assyria, Babylon, Persia, Greece and Rome. Quoting Yirmiyahu, the Midrash says that the message of Yaakov's dream, directed to עם ישראל, is אל תירא עבדי יעקוב, "Fear not, my servant Yaakov" (Yirmiyahu 30:10). It concludes with Ovadyah addressing Edom, "Even if you raise your nest as high as the eagle's, even if you place your nest among the stars, I will bring you down from there" (Ovadyah 1:4). Ovadyah was prophesying about the future fall of Rome, the successor of Edom. The eagle to which Ovadyah refers is most certainly the Roman eagle, the standard symbol of Rome/Edom.

Yaakov's ladder symbolizes the ladder of history. The ascent of one nation can only take place with the descent of its predecessor. However, the ladder is not endless; the Ribono Shel Olam stands at its head as the Master of History, watching over the Jewish people. In this sense, the parashah looks forward to the end of days, when militarism and despotism will be ended and HaShem's sovereignty will be recognized. At that time, the Jewish people will again be in its national home, ארץ ישראל. The prophet Yeshayahu describes אחרית הימים in the 2nd chapter of his prophetic book, "It will be at the end of days: the mountain of the Temple of HaShem will be firmly established, and all the nations will stream to it... [The G-d of Yaakov] will teach us His ways... for from Zion will come the Torah and the word of HaShem from Yerushalayim... They will beat their swords into plowshares... they will no longer study warfare" (Yeshayahu 2:2-4).

Parashas Vayishlach

Parashas Vayishlach is the second parashah in which Yaakov Avinu is the central figure. The parasha continues to relate Yaakov's chronology after leaving his father-in-law, Lavan. Yaakov is now back in his homeland, ארץ ישראל, and his estranged brother, Esav, is approaching. Yaakov prays, "Save me please, from the hand of my brother, from the hand of Esav; for I fear him, lest he come and strike me down, mother and children" (Bereishis 32:12).

Yaakov is terribly worried and afraid of Esav prior to their first meeting after a separation of 20 years. Fearing the worst, Yaakov divides his camp into two, with some of the men, servants and cattle in each group. He keeps the family together in the rear camp, so that the first camp will serve as a buffer between his wives and children, and Esav. If the first camp is overrun, thinks Yaakov, the second camp will continue the battle, והיה המחנה הנשאר לפליטה, and "the remaining camp shall survive" (Bereishis 32:9).

Rashi, commenting on the above verse, explains that Yaakov prepared himself to meet Esav in three ways: לדורון, לתפילה ולמלחמה. First, לדורון, Ya'akov gave herds of cattle and other animals as a "present" to Esav, sent ahead in anticipation of his arrival. Second, לתפילה, Ya'akov prayed to HaShem for salvation. Finally, למלחמה, Ya'akov prepared for battle if diplomacy and prayer did not work.

Rabbi Yitzchak Arama (Spain, 1420-1494), the author of עקידת יצחק, addresses this situation, stating that the Torah commands us to combine faith and prayer with proactive human endeavors. The Gemara (Pesachim 64b) says אין סומכין על הנס, we must not rely solely on miracles. A Jew cannot sit with folded arms when action is required. Just as a person may not give up hope for the future, so is he forbidden to sit idly by when active participation is called for.

The Torah states three times in Devarim (2:7, 14:29 and 15:18) that HaShem blesses our handiwork. In Devarim 15:18, for instance, we read, וברכך ה אלוקיך בכול אשר תעשה, "HaShem will bless you in all that you do." But there is one proviso: A person must act when action is required and only then may he hope that HaShem will bless his actions and that ישועה, salvation, will come from Heaven.

The question then arises, if a person finds himself in a situation in which taking action is impossible, is he then doomed to doing without HaShem's hashgachah (providence)? The answer to this question is to be found in the Gemara, Pesachim 8b, which states, "If one declares this sela (an amount of money) to be for tzedakah, in order that my son may live, he is a tzaddik gamur, a wholly righteous person." On its surface, this statement is surprising. Is it really possible for a person to become a tzaddik merely by donating to charity? The answer is a definite no. Therefore, the only way to understand this statement of the Gemara is to say that the person giving the sela displayed absolute אמונה, faith. He has to believe with all his heart that צדקה תציל ממות, "tzedakah saves from death" (Mishlei 10:2). As we say during the Yamim Noraim, ותשובה, ותפילה, וצדקה מעבירין את רוע הגזרה, "Repentance, prayer and charity remove the evil of the decree." It is this absolute belief that makes him a tzaddik gamur, a wholly righteous man.

It is worth noting that tzedakah includes not only what one gives to the poor, but also support one gives to students of Torah and yeshivos.

Following the descriptions of Yaakov's anxiety and subsequent prayer, we are introduced to another subject – Yaakov's struggle with an angel. This is a most mysterious and mystical event. How do we understand the concept of a man struggling with a Divine angel? The angel wrestles with Yaakov, and Yaakov's hip is dislocated. The angel then gives Yaakov a new name, Yisrael, כי שרית עם אלוקים ועם אנשים ותוכל, "because you struggled with the Divine and with man, and you have overcome" (Bereishis 32:29). Yaakov's new name vindicates him, changing him from the younger son grabbing the heel of his older brother to a worthy patriarch endeavoring to fulfill his calling. The angel's blessing of Yaakov confirms him as the rightful recipient of the blessing he received from his father, Yitzchak.

This episode was HaShem's answer to Yaakov's plea for protection from Esav's wrath. Yaakov prayed, הצילני נא (Bereishis 32:12), "Please save me" and my family and all of כלל ישראל. We know that HaShem answered him positively, saying, in effect: Since you proactively prepared your camps to withstand a battle with Esav, and since you struggled with the angel, you deserve that your prayers be answered fully. Esav will never destroy you, your family or the nation of Israel."

As confirmation of the angel's blessing of perpetual continuity for עם ישראל, right after the struggle with the angel we read that ויזרח לו השמש, "the sun rose for him" (Bereishis 32:32). The sun is eternal, rising every single day that the Earth exists. So, too, will Israel continue to exist until the end of days, for Israel is עם הנצח, the eternal nation.

Parashas Vayeishev

In the book of Bereishis, two parshiyos are dedicated to each of the main characters. Yosef is the central figure in Parashas Vayeishev, as well as in Parashas Miketz, to be read next week. This essay discusses the saga of Yosef, his unique place in the Torah and his worldly and spiritual achievements.

To understand Yosef's greatness, we must first consider the three blessings he received, two from Yaakov before he died (Bereishis 48:15-16 and Bereishis 49:22-26) and one from Moshe before בני ישראל entered the Holy Land (Devarim 33:13-18). It is clear that the blessings of Yosef and his descendents are superior to those given to the other sons of Yaakov and confirm the special place that Yosef held amongst his 11 brothers.

However, Yosef did not attain the madregah, the level, of his father, whom the rabbis of the Midrash declared to be בחיר האבות, the chosen of the Patriarchs (Tanchuma, Miketz 12). Yaakov dreamed of angels and HaShem spoke to him and blessed him. Yosef is in a category of his own. Whilst HaShem never spoke to Yosef, he lived both as the favored son of the last of the three אבות and, at the same time, as the father of two of the 12 tribes (Targum Onkelos).

Yaakov loved Yosef more than his other sons because Yosef was one of his last born, the child of his old age (Bereishis 37:3). He transmitted to Yosef the legacy of Shem, as Rashi informs us, quoting the Midrash, "Whatever Yaakov had learned from Shem and Ever, he transmitted to Yosef" (Rashi on Bereishis 37:3). Shem was the son of Noach, and the father of the Semitic branch of mankind and, like his father, he was also a tzaddik. The legacy of Shem was the belief in one G-d, Creator of the world and all mankind, and acceptance of the validity of the seven mitzvos Bnei Noach (Noahide Laws), which include prohibitions against murder, theft and sexual immorality. Shem also accepted the mandate to live with all people in love and harmony and to conduct himself with honesty and integrity.

Yosef followed these universal principles but, in addition, he was fully committed to the destiny of בני ישראל to achieve nationhood in ארץ ישראל.

Yosef followed the teachings of Shem that are based only on גשמיות, a worldly view of life, a perspective crucial to his successful implementation of the food-rationing plan in Egypt (Bereishis 41). But his father Yaakov believed that life must focus also on רוחניות, spiritual values. Yaakov, as we know, married two sisters, Rachel who, like Avraham, understood the earthly aspects of life, and Leah who, like Yitzchak, was absolutely focused on the spiritual. Yosef followed in the footsteps of his mother, Rachel.

Yosef had an inborn talent to understand עולם הזה, the affairs of this world. He was not like Yehudah, a man centered in Torah and spirituality who opened a yeshivah when Yaakov, with his family of 70 souls, came to Egypt. Yosef was beloved by all who came into contact with him, as we read, וימצא יוסף חן בעיניו, "and Yosef found favor in his eyes" (Bereishis 39:4).

When Yosef became lost on his way to Shechem, a man – whom Rashi says was the angel Gavriel – directed him to Dotan, to his brothers' camp. It was at this point that Yosef realized that Divine Providence was guiding his life and that HaShem had bestowed a mission upon him. Later, Yosef realized that his mission was to help fulfill the covenant that HaShem had made with Avraham.

In rejecting the advances of Potiphar's wife, Yosef said that, were he to lie with her, וחטאתי לאלוקים, "I will have sinned against HaShem" (Bereishis 39:9). Yosef's resistance to temptation in this affair is seen in our tradition as the supreme example of chastity and he is, consequently, called "Yosef haTzaddik." Indeed, Yosef is the only Jewish person named a צדיק in the entire Tanach. In fact, the prophet Amos refers to him as such. In the haftarah for Parashas Vayeishev, Amos prophesies, "Should I not exact retribution... for their having sold a tzaddik for silver and a destitute one for the sake of a pair of shoes" (Amos 2:6)?

The *Zohar*, too, considers Yosef a true tzaddik; not like Shem and Ever, but a Jewish tzaddik. Indeed, the *Zohar* places him among the seven אושפיזין, spiritual guests, who visit the סוכה. The אושפיזין arrive in the following order, one on each of the seven days of Sukkos: Avraham, Yitzchak, Yaakov, Moshe, Aharon, Yosef and David. In the *Zohar*, Yosef represents the ספירה of יסוד, foundation, the source of all cosmic energy, represented by the organ of generation in the human body. In kabbalistic order, יסוד comes before מלכות, kingship, because מלכות can only come from יסוד. This is why Yosef visits the סוכה immediately before King David.

Yosef was a man who achieved greatness by being of this mundane, physical world. In doing so, he played a crucial role in the physical and spiritual betterment of the Jewish people and mankind. At the end of days, Mashiach ben Yosef will lay the practical groundwork for the return of the Jewish people to ארץ ישראל in preparation for the arrival of Mashiach ben David.

Parashas Mikeitz

Parashas Mikeitz continues the story of Yosef and his brothers. While Parashas Vayeishev described Yosef's dreams, Parashas Mikeitz describes their effects on Yosef's life. In chapter 42, we read that, as a result of the famine in Canaan, Yaakov instructed his sons to go down to Egypt to purchase food. Upon arrival, they encountered their lost brother Yosef, who, the Torah tells us, "acted like a stranger towards them and spoke with them harshly" (Bereishis 42:7). ויכר יוסף את אחיו והם לא הכרוהו, "Yosef recognized them, but they did not recognize him" (Bereishis 42:8). Yosef sternly accused them, saying, אתם מרגלים, "you are spies" (Bereishis 42:9).

More than 20 years had passed since Yosef's descent into captivity in Egypt, yet he remained possessed by the dreams he had dreamed at the age of 17. We recall that the young Yosef had two dreams of personal greatness, the first in which his brothers' sheaves bowed down to his sheaf; and the second in which the sun, the moon and 11 stars bowed down to him.

The Ramban explains that when Yosef saw only 10 of his brothers before him, he immediately understood that it would be impossible for his dreams to become a reality without the presence of Binyamin, the 11th brother, who had remained in Canaan with Yaakov. Furthermore, fulfillment of his second dream required Yaakov's presence in Egypt. The sun in Yosef's dream is, of course, Yaakov and the stars are his brothers. Since his mother Rachel had died entering ארץ ישראל, prior to Yosef's descent to Egypt, Leah could perhaps have taken on the role of the moon.

In addition, the Ramban writes that the importance of Yosef actualizing his dreams justifies the great pain he caused his father. By not sending word to Canaan that he was alive, he prolonged Yaakov's mourning for the son he thought had been devoured by a חיה רעה, a wild beast. Quoting the verse in Koheles (3:1), לכל זמן ועת לכל חפץ תחת השמים, "everything has its season, and there is a time for everything under heaven," the

Ramban comments, "[Yosef] assigned each to its proper time in order to fulfill the dreams, knowing that they would truly be fulfilled."

This justification of Yosef's harsh behavior towards his father aroused tremendous opposition from Rabbi Yitzchak Arama, the author of עקידת יצחק. Arama, who lived in Spain in the 15th century, asks, "What did Yosef have to gain from turning his dreams into reality? Even if he had derived some benefit, he should not have sinned against his own father." Arama concludes that He who causes humans to dream – that is, HaShem – will also provide their solution. The actualization of dreams is not the responsibility of dreamers.

The Jewish people have always dreamed. Take, for example, Shir Hamaalot, "שיר המעלות בשוב ה את שיבת ציון היינו כחולמים A song of ascents; when HaShem will return the captivity of Zion, we will be like dreamers" (Tehillim 126:1). However, in the case of the dreams of Yosef, while the Ramban justified Yosef's behavior as entirely necessary to bring about their actualization, Arama criticizes his insistence on fulfilling them at the price of causing pain to his father. In his behavior in Egypt, writes Arama, Yosef did not fulfil the mitzvah that we now know as כיבוד אב ואם, honor thy father and thy mother.

According to Koheles (7:20), אין צדיק בארץ אשר יעשה טוב ולא יחטא, "There is no man so wholly righteous on Earth that always does good and never sins." Yosef was a tzaddik. The previous parashah, Vayeishev, states that Yosef is the only Jew explicitly described as a tzaddik. Like all tzaddikim who want to do good, including Moshe Rabbenu, he erred, says Arama, his deception of Yaakov was the error.

Every generation has its dreams and its dreamers. Rav Kook expresses this idea in poetic form in his book, *Igeres HaKodesh*, "Great dreams are the foundation of the world itself... It is through dreams that HaShem spoke to His prophets, בחלום אדבר בו, 'in a dream I shall speak to him' (Bamidbar 12:6). And dreamers of great ideas speak of תיקון עולם, 'repairing the world.' " Yosef was a great dreamer but, in this case, Rishonim disagree in their evaluation of his behavior. Arama points out how Yosef caused pain to Yaakov. The Ramban's view is that Yosef indeed did the right thing at the right time.

Shabbos Chanukah (Mikeitz)

Chanukah, like Purim, is a חג that was instituted by the תנאים, Tannaim. While the story of Purim is narrated in Megillas Esther, which is part of the 24 holy books of the תני״ך, Chanukah is narrated in the Gemara. In terms of halachah, however, both fall into the category of מצוות דרבנן, post-Biblical commandments established by חז״ל.

The Gemara says in Shabbos 21b, מאי חנוכה, "What is the reason for Chanukah? On the 25th day of Kislev, commence the days of Chanukah, which are eight (days) on which lamentation for the dead and fasting are forbidden. The Greeks entered the Beis Hamikdash and defiled all the oils they found there. When the Hasmonean dynasty defeated the Greeks, they searched and found only one container of pure oil with the seal of the כהן גדול, which contained sufficient (oil) for one day's lighting only. Then a miracle happened. They lit the menorah and it lasted for eight days. The following year, these days were appointed as a festival, with Hallel and thanksgiving."

The text of this passage of the Gemara is taken verbatim from מגילת תענית, a document written in Aramaic dating from the 1st century C.E. It contains a list of the days on which fasting is prohibited due to the good fortunes of the Jewish people on those days. Chanukah is clearly noted as the festival celebrating the great miracle that HaShem made with the oil so that the Beis Hamikdash could be rededicated to HaShem and the קרבנות, the sacrificial services, reinstated. Only a few words in מגלית תענית describe the miraculous military victory of the Hasmoneans over the mighty Greek army.

Focusing on the miracle of the oil, the תנאים realized that the Roman authorities would not tolerate the Jews celebrating their victory over the Greeks, despite that victory having occurred 200 to 300 years earlier. They would also be concerned because of the recent Bar Kochba revolt against Roman occupation, in 132 C.E. For these reasons, the festival of Chanukah was hardly mentioned in the Mishnah. It was certainly the reason that the

תנאים declared Chanukah a religious holiday since the festival was in remembrance of the miracle of the oil used for the sanctification of the Beis Hamikdash.

In about 750 C.E., a new prayer, על הנסים, for the miracles, was added, to be recited during the eight days of Channukah. Authorship of this prayer is attributed to Rabbi Achai (8th century Bavel and ארץ ישראל), who was the greatest sage during the period of the Saboraim, the rabbis who flourished after the Talmudic era. In this prayer, the miracle is identified not only with the oil but also with the great military victory in which HaShem delivered the strong into the hands of the weak, the many into the hands of the few. The prayer concludes, "They appointed these eight days of Chanukah in order to give thanks and praise unto Your great name."

The Saboraim understood that the war against the Greeks was not purely for military or political reasons, but to secure the supremacy of Torah over Hellenism. It was a war between two opposing cultures. It was a war fought to reestablish Torah and tradition and to assure the spiritual purity of Jewish life in ארץ ישראל. The reason for this war resonates even today. It was a war for קידוש השם and finds expression when we light the menorah and say בימים ההם בזמן הזה, in those days and in our time.

The Saboraim, then, shifted the focus from the miracle of the oil to the miracle of victory on the battlefield. In על הנסים, they added that HaShem "delivered the impure into the hands of the pure, the wicked into the hands of the righteous, and the arrogant into the hands of those who occupy themselves with Torah." The Maccabean revolt was a war for Torah values; in fact, it was the first religious war in world history. Centuries later, the Rambam in the "Laws of Chanukah" in his *Mishneh Torah* takes the same approach, giving equal expression to the miracle of the war as he gives to the miracle of the oil.

In the 16th century, the Maharal of Prague, in his book נר חנוכה, *The Light of Chanukah*, offers a new understanding of whether the dominant miracle of Chanukah was the oil or the war. Both, he said, had great value, but for different reasons. He states, "Therefore, the miracle was performed through the light of the menorah, that all should understand that everything comes about as a miracle from HaShem. So, also, the victory of the battlefield was a miracle from Heaven."

Sadly, the kings of the Hasmonean dynasty abandoned the spiritual values they had cherished when they fought against the Hellenistic enemy. In the wake of their abandonment, their political and military achievements were short-lived. However, the spiritual values of Chanukah, the victory of the pure over the impure, light over darkness, remain for generations to celebrate. The Chanukah lights have guided the Jewish people in overcoming all adversities. They have guided us in our times, with the great miracle of the establishment of the State of Israel and flourishing Torah study. The State of Israel has continually been victorious in battle and the Chanukah lights will continue to guide us until the end of days, the Days of Mashiach.

Parashas Vayigash

Yosef is again the central personality in this week's parashah. After bringing his father Yaakov, together with his entire family of 70 souls to Egypt, he settles them in a separate area called Goshen. Having reconciled with his brothers, Yosef remains devoted to them, helping and protecting them. At the same time, he serves as viceroy of Egypt. Having interpreted Pharaoh's dreams predicting seven years of bounty followed by seven years of famine, Yosef saves Egypt from the famine. The Torah presents Yosef as extremely capable and successful in all matters of עולם הזה, the physical world. He excels in economics, agriculture, psychology and the interpretation of dreams. Yet Yosef thinks and acts in conformity with Torah values, despite having lived 400 years before the Torah was given at Sinai.

We read in the parashah, "Yosef sustained his father and his brothers and all of his father's household with food according to the number of children" (Bereishis 47:12). Yosef instinctively fulfilled the fifth commandment, "Honor your father and mother," which the Ramban says includes nourishing them. This is also the Rambam's position in Hilchos Mamrim (6:5). Furthermore, by sustaining his brothers, Yosef anticipated Yeshayahu's admonition, "Surely, you break your bread with the hungry... ומבשרך לא תתעלם, and do not hide from your kin" (Yeshayahu 58:7). Even today, this principle is still adhered to and is found in Hilchos Tzedakah of Yoreh Deah in the Shulchan Aruch.

Yosef himself observed meticulously the regulations for rationing that he had ordered during the famine. He refused to increase the rations of his brothers' families, which would have constituted favoritism. Rather, he distributed food strictly in accordance with the number of children in each family. Yosef did not exploit his position for personal enrichment. The text of the parashah explains that he collected all the money held by the people of the lands of Egypt and Canaan and, in exchange, sold them grain. The Torah then confirms that Yosef handed over all the wealth he collected to the house of Pharaoh

(Bereishis 47:14). Yosef conducted his administration as viceroy of Egypt ביושר ובצדק, with honesty and with justice. Furthermore, he carried out his duties with compassion; there was no hint of nepotism or corruption.

When the famine worsened, the Egyptians pleaded, "Buy us and our land for bread, and we, with our land, will become serfs to Pharaoh" (Bereishis 47:19). But Yosef accepted only their land and turned down their offer to become enslaved to Pharaoh. The parashah tells us, "Yosef bought all the land of Egypt for Pharaoh, for every Egyptian sold his field because the famine had overwhelmed them" (Bereishis 47:20). It was a nationalization of the land but not of the people. In addition, Yosef demanded of the newly-made sharecroppers only 20 percent of their future harvests as payment to Pharaoh. The Egyptians expressed their thanks when they exclaimed, החיתנו, "You have saved our lives" (Bereishis 47:25).

In this parashah, we see that Yosef's views on slavery are associated with those expressed in the Torah, which clearly opposes complete subjugation of servants. In Parashas Behar, in Sefer Vayikra, HaShem instructs בני ישראל in the laws of dealing with kinsmen who find themselves in such dire financial circumstances that they must hire themselves out as servants. According to the Torah, they need to be treated well and viewed as indentured servants who will spend only a limited number of years with their masters (Vayikra 25:50-55), כי לי בני ישראל עבדים, "For it is to Me that the Israelites are servants, they are My servants, whom I freed from the land of Egypt" (Vayikra 25:55). Yosef anticipates this attitude by refusing to turn free men into slaves in their own land.

Yosef's behavior is focused on עולם הזה, as revealed to us by his preoccupation with the physical welfare of his brothers and the laws he introduces as viceroy of Egypt. Yosef embodies the here-and-now, and it is this attitude that חז"ל ascribe to Mashiach ben Yosef. Yosef followed in the footsteps of his mother Rachel, who was also centered in עולם הזה, the earthly aspects of life, in contrast to her sister Leah, who was the embodiment of the spiritual.

The Gemara (Sukkah 52a-b) states that Mashiach ben Yosef will appear before Mashiach ben David, in order to prepare ארץ ישראל for the ingathering of the exiles and provide for their physical needs. He will raise a Jewish army to defend the Land against the enemies of עם ישראל and the Land will respond with bounty. Only then will Mashiach ben David hasten our spirtual redemption, will prophecy reappear, and will the Beis Hamikdash be reestablished.

The commentary *Kol HaTor*, written in the late 18th century by Rav Hillel Shklover (which is addended to Rav Menachem Kasher's book, *Hatekufah Hagedolah* [1969]), interprets the Vilna Gaon on the *Zohar* on Parashas Vayera to understand that we are now in the period of ימות המשיח, the Messianic Age. In last week's parashah we read, ויכר יוסף את אחיו והם לא הכרהו, "Yosef recognized his brothers but they did not recognize him" (Bereishis 42:8). When Mashiach ben Yosef appears, he will recognize his brothers. However, says the Vilna Gaon, they will not recognize him, or even recognize that they are living in the era of ימות המשיח. It is reasonable to conclude, whether we recognize it or not, that we are currently living in that period.

Parashas Vayechi

Parashas Vayechi concludes the book of Bereishis. Chapter 49 begins, ויקרא יעקב אל בניו, "Yaakov called for his sons and said, 'Assemble yourselves, and I will tell you what will befall you באחרית הימים, in the end of days'" (Bereishis 49:1). Rashi, quoting the Gemara (Pesachim 56a) and the Midrash (Bereishis Raba 89:5), writes that Yaakov intended to reveal what would happen באחרית הימים but ונסתלקה ממנו השכינה, the Divine Presence left him. Therefore, although Yaakov Avinu was a נביא, at that moment he could not prophesy ימות המשיח, the Messianic Age, and focused instead on the characters of the fathers of the 12 tribes and how they would manifest in the history of בני ישראל.

There is a dispute between Abarbanel (15th century) and other Rishonim regarding the intent and purpose of Yaakov's monologue to his sons. Most of the Rishonim believe that Yaakov's words should be considered ברכות, blessings, to those who were worthy and תוכחות, rebukes, to those who were not. Abarbanel, in a lengthy dissertation, claims that Yaakov's words must be understood as נבואה, prophetic statements intended to reveal which brother and which tribe would generate Israel's leaders. In other words, Yaakov's purpose was to establish a clear line of succession, thereby averting quarrels between the tribes and ensuring that Israel would have worthy leaders.

According to Abarbanel, because of HaShem's blessings to Yaakov, he knew that the 12 tribes would develop into a great and holy nation and would eventually need kings to rule over them. Yaakov therefore probed the behavior and analyzed the character traits of each of his 12 sons, knowing that their personalities and characteristics would be passed on to their descendants. The sons of Yaakov were apprehensive that their father's last words would make explicit his disapproval of their sins and failings. The Midrash describes Yehudah's unease when he approached his father: "When Yaakov mentioned the failures of Reuven and Shimon, Yehudah became pale; he was terrified that he would be censured for his sexual encounter with Tamar" (Yalkut Shimoni 159).

The brothers' apprehensions were not without basis, for Yaakov's words to his sons were unsparing. Reuven was disqualified because, in the words of Yaakov, he was פחז כמים אל תותר כי עלית משכבי אביך, "impetuous as water; you cannot be foremost, because you mounted your father's bed" (Bereishis 49:4). חז"ל explain that, after Rachel's death, Yaakov slept in the tent of Bilhah, Rachel's maidservant. Reuven considered this an affront to his mother and therefore, without permission, moved Yaakov's bed to the tent of Leah. In doing so, Reuven fulfilled the mitzvah of כיבוד אם but dishonored his father and failed in the mitzvah of כיבוד אב. Shimon and Levi were disqualified because כלי חמס מכרותיהם, "weapons of violence are their stolen craft" (Bereishis 49:5). They had killed the males of Shechem, and men of the sword are unworthy of the throne. In the words of Mishlei (29:4), מלך במשפט יעמיד ארץ, "Only through justice does a king establish a land."

All of the other sons of Yaakov, with the exception of Yehudah, had displayed failures of character and were therefore disqualified for כתר מלכות, the crown of royalty. Yaakov considered Yehudah to be the most qualified of his sons to establish Israel's future royal dynasty and he blessed Yehudah, saying, "Your brothers will acknowledge you; your hand will be at your enemies' nape; your father's sons will prostrate themselves to you" (Bereishis 49:8). By declaring, לא יסור שבט מיהודה, "The scepter shall not depart from Yehudah, nor a scholar from among his descendants," Yaakov assigned to Yehudah the crown of kingship and made the house of Yehudah the source of leadership for the Jewish people. Yaakov said, עד כי יבוא שילה, "until Shiloh arrives," which, states Rashi, quoting Onkelos and the midrashim, is referring to Mashiach, who will appear at the end of days (Bereishis 49:10).

Abarbanel emphasizes that Yaakov's blessings are not arbitrary or personal, for otherwise he would have conferred the kingship upon Yosef, whom he loved more than Yehudah; or he would have appointed Binyamin, the youngest son of his beloved wife Rachel. In his blessings, Yaakov, the founding father of the nation, admits that Yosef is lacking in royal qualities. As we read, וימררהו ורבו וישטמהו בעלי חצים, "They embittered him and became antagonists; the arrow-tongued men hated him" (Bereishis 49:23). He who is hated by his brothers, Abarbanel explains, cannot become their king.

An interesting question arises: Why did Yaakov bless Yosef with five psukim of ברכות and Yehudah with only four? Abarbanel explains that, "As HaShem did not destine Yosef to become king, Yaakov bestowed many other blessings upon him," blessings that Yosef richly deserved because of all the good he had brought to the family of Yaakov. Yaakov's blessings to Yosef bespeak the profound affection and love he felt for Rachel's older son. However, as the forefather of the nation, Yaakov finds him wanting as a leader, and thus, in an act of נבואה, he confers the leadership of Israel on his most worthy son, Yehudah.

In conclusion, most of the Rishonim believed that Yaakov, before his death, assembled his 12 sons in order to bestow blessing on those deserving and rebuke on those who had failed. Abarbanel, a seasoned advisor to the kings of Portugal, Spain and Naples, saw things differently. He understood that Yaakov addressed his sons primarily to explain why Yehudah had been chosen as Israel's king-elect, his descendents to govern Israel until the end of days. Both interpretations contain valuable insights for our reading of the Torah.

2 SEFER SHEMOS

Parashas Shemos

The Book of שמות describes the history of בני ישראל in Egypt but, more importantly, it introduces us to קדושת ישראל, the sanctity of the Jewish people. The parashah begins by stating that Yaakov and his entire family, the 70 souls, died in Egypt, וימת יוסף וכל אחיו וכל הדור ההוא, "Yosef died, and all his brothers, and that entire generation" (Shemos 1:6). The founding fathers of the Jewish people and their families, of whom we read in Bereishis, passed away and were replaced by an amorphous multitude of people who, at the time of the Exodus, numbered 600,000 adult men. In this parashah, Pharaoh is the first to recognize Israel's nationhood by saying, הנה עם בני ישראל, "Behold, the nation of the Children of Israel" (Shemos 1:9).

As stated in Parashas Lech Lecha, the Maharal of Prague (16th century) expresses a fascinating insight in his book נצח ישראל, *The Eternity of Israel*. He writes, השם יתברך בחר בישראל בעצם ולא בשביל מעשיהם הטובים, "HaShem, may He be Blessed, chose Israel in and of themselves and not because of any of their good deeds" (chapter 11). This is a reminder of the way in which the Torah introduces Avraham Avinu. The Torah does not call Avraham a tzaddik, a righteous person, as it does with Noach (compare Bereishis 6:9 and 12:1). The Maharal concludes that HaShem selected Avraham, not because of his personal righteousness – of which Avraham was greatly possessed – but because he was destined to be the progenitor of the holy nation, Israel. In this way, as the descendants of Avraham, we – the Jewish people – have an inherent, immutable kedushah. As individuals, we must strive to improve our own personal deeds for which only we are responsible, but HaShem wanted a nation that is absolutely, inherently holy and Avraham was the means for the creation of that holy nation.

In next week's parashah, HaShem confirms that Israel had become a nation in Egypt by instructing Moshe to tell Pharaoh, שלח את עמי, "Let my nation go" (Shemos 7:26). At that moment, בני ישראל became not only a nation but rather His people, the holy nation. Since then, the Jewish people have embodied קדושת ישראל, the inherent sanctity of the nation of Israel. In Sefer Bereishis, we find Noach, Shem, Ever and Hanoch, who were all righteous men. Therefore, חז"ל stated that "the righteous among the nations of the world" can "share in the world to come" (Tosefta Sanhedrin 13). But they were all individuals; only individuals among the אומות העולם can merit עולם הבא. Israel is the only nation that is holy in its identity as a nation. This is confirmed in Shemos 19:6, ואתם תהיו לי ממלכת כהנים וגוי קדוש, "You will be for Me a kingdom of priests and a holy nation." עם ישראל, as such, is holy.

The concept of קדושת ישראל, the holiness of Israel, is expressed in the Gemara (Berachos 60b), which is included in our daily prayers, "My God, the soul you have placed in me is pure. You created it, You fashioned it, You breathed it into me." Similarly, the *Zohar* comments on the pasuk in the story of Creation, ויפח באפיו נשמת חיים, "and He blew into his nostrils the soul of life" (Bereishis 2:7), saying "the One who blows, blows from within Himself." In other words, G-dliness resides within every Jewish person.

The way HaShem's kedushah manifests in Parashas Shemos teaches us many things. At the Burning Bush, HaShem tells Moshe, "Remove your shoes from your feet, for the place upon which you stand is אדמת קודש, holy ground" (Shemos 3:5). Here, the Torah confirms that HaShem's kedushah is present within the bush itself, והנה הסנה בער באש והסנה איננו אכל, "The bush was burning in the fire, but the bush was not consumed" (Shemos 3:2).

The Midrash offers us a number of possible interpretations of the meaning of the Burning Bush. According to a story told in Shemos Rabbah 2:5, "A certain heathen asked R. Yehoshua b.

Korcha, 'What prompted the Holy One Blessed Be He to speak to Moshe from the thorn-bush?' The answer given is, to teach us that אין שכינה בלא פנוי מקום, "There is no place without the Divine Presence, not even a thorn-bush." This midrash became the focal point of a dispute between the Hasidim and the Misnagdim at the beginning of the 19th century. The Hasidim understood the midrash to mean that the שכינה, the Divine Presence, is to be found in the bad as well as the good. According to this point of view, the שכינה resides in every Jewish person at every moment, whether he or she is committing an act that is permitted or one that is forbidden. This idea is to be found in the book דגל מחנה אפרים, *The Standard of the Camp of Ephraim*, written by the grandson of the Baal Shem Tov. Even if a person commits a sin, the שכינה is there with him, for without the שכינה he would not be able to function or even to exist.

Nechama Leibowitz, a 20th century scholar from Israel, writes in *Studies in Shemos*, that since the days of Philo (1st century C.E.), "the frail bush has been understood as the symbol of puny Israel threatened with destruction by the fire of Egyptian persecution." The midrash spells this out, "Why did the Holy One Blessed Be He, formulate His revelation in this manner? Because Moshe was afraid that the Egyptians would really destroy Israel. Accordingly, the Holy One Blessed Be He showed him a burning bush, which was never consumed. He said to him, 'Just as the bush burns with fire but is never consumed, Egypt will never destroy Israel.'" The French Torah commentator R. Chizkiyah Chizkuni (13th century) makes the same point, stating that just as the fire could not burn the bush, so the enemies of Israel will never destroy the Jewish people. Even today, the fires of the Holocaust could not extinguish the Jewish people.

In conclusion, Parashas Shemos teaches us that the Jewish people are possessed of a distinct and inherent sanctity, קדושת ישראל. HaShem chose us and as He and His kedushah are eternal, so are His people, the Am Kadosh.

Parashas Va'eira

This week's parashah opens with the words, "HaShem spoke to Moshe and said, 'I am HaShem,' Yud-Heh-Vav-Heh. I appeared to Avraham, to Yitzchak and to Yaakov as El Shaddai, but with my name HaShem, I did not make myself known to them'" (Shemos 6:2-3).

Why did HaShem not reveal His holiest name to the אבות, forefathers? In Sefer Bereishis, HaShem is mentioned by different names but it is to Moshe that He first reveals Himself by His eternal ineffable Name, whose essence cannot be described by human beings. In Hebrew the name is spelled Yud-Heh-Vav-Heh, but because it is too sacred to be pronounced, we use "HaShem (the Name)" in its place. The four-letter name is utterly holy because these four Hebrew letters convey the essence of HaShem, in contrast to the many names one is permitted to pronounce, which are descriptive, or attribute qualities to Him – for instance, El Shaddai, "G-d who sets limits." Contained in the letters Yud-Heh-Vav-Heh are the words היה, הווה and יהיה, past, present, and future. HaShem existed before time, exists now and will exist forever. He is timeless. He is at once present here and is beyond time, immanent and transcendent. He has no limitations.

The Ramban explains that El Shaddai describes HaShem when He performs miracles that do not openly contradict the normal course of nature. This reflects the way the אבות perceived HaShem; He assured their survival in times of famine, He gave them victories over superior enemies, and He assured them of success in all their undertakings. The אבות displayed extraordinary faith in HaShem and, therefore, did not need supernatural miracles to support their אמונה. In contrast, Moshe and בני ישראל did not display the great faith of their forefathers. It is for this reason that they were in need of נסים גלויים, supernatural miracles that were obvious and overwhelming. The view expressed by the Ramban is that the faith of the אבות was simpler and purer than that of Moshe Rabbeinu, who was sometimes overcome with despair and needed miracles that were clearly supernatural in order to bolster his faith; for instance the Burning Bush, the plagues, the parting of the Red Sea, and the daily appearance of manna.

Rabbi Yehuda Halevi (d. mid-12th century), in his book *The Kuzari*, proposed a different interpretation than that of the Ramban. He said that it was not because the אבות were in any way superior in their faith, or that Moshe was inferior to them. Rather, the אבות were select יחידים, individuals, with whom HaShem communicated directly; it was not necessary for Him to make His presence and power known through miracles and wonders. But in the days of Moshe, בני ישראל were numerous and their faith was weak because they had been terribly oppressed for generations. They had forgotten the traditions of the אבות. They were not able to appreciate hidden miracles unaccompanied by an obvious change in the natural order. To be convinced of HaShem's greatness, they needed a display of the supernatural. That is why they were brought out of Egypt with what the Torah describes as a yad chazakah, a "strong hand." For this reason, the אבות could perceive HaShem without the ineffable name and without supernatural miracles, whereas Moshe and his generation required both.

Further insight into the question of why HaShem did not reveal His name to the אבות can be found in the prayer, ובא לציון גואל, "And a redeemer shall come to Zion," which we recite every day. This prayer was composed before the period of the Tannaim, and is perhaps the oldest of our prayers. It was named Kedushah d'Sidra, translated by Rashi as "the order of sanctity" in his commentary on the Gemara (Sotah 49a). In the Talmudic era, a verse was added to the prayer from Yeshayahu 6:3 "Kadosh, kadosh, kadosh," including its Aramaic translation. This was because בני ישראל at that time – like the Jews in the generation of Moshe – had lost the tradition and forgotten Hebrew, and the words were therefore translated so that they could understand their sacred meaning. In Hebrew, the pasuk reads, קדוש קדוש קדוש ה צבאות מלא כל הארץ כבודו, "Holy, holy,

holy is HaShem, Master of Legions; the whole world is filled with His Glory." The Aramaic translation and interpretation reads, "HaShem, Master of Legions, is holy in three different realms: Holy in the most exalted heaven, the abode of His Presence; holy on Earth, product of His strength; holy forever and ever."

This prayer is central to our concept of HaShem because it emphasizes that HaShem is present in the upper world as well as the lower world, and that He is eternal. Our sages state that the essence of HaShem, expressed in Yud-Heh-Vav-Heh, is the source of kedushah, holiness, in the world. This is the significance of the words Ani HaShem, "I am HaShem," that appear in the first verse of this week's parashah.

HaShem revealed His ineffable Name during the arduous process of freeing בני ישראל from their enslavement in Egypt. At the same time, He confirmed the nationhood of Israel by instructing Moshe to go to Pharaoh and demand, שלח את עמי, "Let my people go" (Shemos 5:1). During their sojourn in Egypt, the sons of Yaakov had become the nation of בני ישראל. The אבות did not encounter HaShem through the ineffable Name, but Moshe Rabbeinu and his generation did. When HaShem revealed His name to Moshe, Ani HaShem, then בני ישראל could begin a life of kedushah, filled with יראת שמים, piety and אהבת ה׳, the love of HaShem.

Parashas Bo

Parashas Bo tells the history of the Jewish people in Egypt during the period of the last three plagues and the beginning of the Exodus. The first part of the parashah is a description of events, while the second part includes the first מצוות, commandments, in the Torah. Most of them are related to what is known as Pesach Mitzrayim, the first Pesach in Jewish history, which took place in Egypt.

It is no coincidence that the holiday of Pesach is named after Pesach Mitzrayim, as the pasuk states, HaShem pasach – "passed over" – the houses of the Israelites (Shemos 12:13). This "passing over" is the central event of יציאת מצרים, the Exodus from Egypt, and is crucial to our understanding both of this parashah and the holiday of Pesach.

The Rambam (12th century), in *Moreh Nevuchim*, the *Guide to the Perplexed*, writes that the Egyptians were accustomed to worshipping Taleh, which is Aries, the Zodiac sign of the lamb, whose month corresponds with Nisan, when the events of this parashah take place. In response to the idolatry of the Egyptians, בני ישראל were commanded to perform Pesach Mitzrayim – that is, to slaughter a lamb and sprinkle its blood on their doorposts.

The Rambam believed that, in Egypt, בני ישראל were deeply implicated in avodah zarah, idol worship, although the Torah makes no mention of this. He saw Pesach Mitzrayim as an act of תשובה, repentence, for having adopted Egyptian ways, an act that transformed בני ישראל into baalei teshuvah, those who have repented their sins. The Rambam's position is based on a midrash concerning this parashah. R. Yossi ha-Glili, a Tanna, interprets Moshe's command to the people, משכו וקחו לכם צאן, "draw forth or buy for yourselves lambs" (Shemos 12:21), to mean, "draw out your hands from idolatry and cleave to the commandments" (cf. Mechilta, 74). He thus implies that, while in Egypt, בני ישראל had engaged in avodah zarah. According to the Rambam, the purpose of Pesach Mitzrayim was two-fold: so that בני ישראל would cleanse themselves of Egyptian idolatry, and demonstrate publicly their rejection of pagan Egyptian customs.

Rabbi Yaakov Tzvi Mecklenburg (1785-1865), the Rav of Koenigsburg, then also known as Danzig (now Gdansk, Poland), and the author of *הכתב והקבלה*, *The Written Torah and the Oral Law*, agreed with the Rambam on this matter. In his opinion, the three-fold ceremony of the Paschal lamb — dedicating, slaughtering and then painting the blood on the doorposts, not secretly but in public — constituted an act of true teshuvah. The Mecklenburger concludes by quoting Rashi's comment on a pasuk from Parashas Bo, והיה הדם לכם לאת, "the blood shall be a sign for you" (Shemos 12:13). The blood, Rashi writes, was a symbol for בני ישראל of their own teshuvah, not a sign intended to convey a message to anyone else.

Both the Rambam and the Mecklenburger consider the purpose of Pesach Mitzrayim to effect a change in the outlook of בני ישראל. However, whereas the Rambam stressed the liberation of their minds from superstition through teshuvah in an act of ruchanius (spirituality), the Mecklenburger declared that their release from living in fear of their Egyptian taskmasters was a supreme act of mesiras nefesh, self-sacrifice, which is part of gashmius, the physicality of this world.

One aspect of Pesach Mitzrayim needs further elucidation. "HaShem... will see the blood [of the lamb] that is on the lintel and the two doorposts, and HaShem will pass over the entrance and He will not permit המשחית, the Destroyer, to enter your homes to smite" (Shemos 12:23).

Who, then, is the משחית, the Destroyer? The Vilna Gaon is credited with the explanation that, on the night of Pesach, the real משחית, the Angel of Death, would be held back by HaShem, and no Jew would die. On that night, they did not say Krias Shema as part of the bedtime prayer. The eve of the first day of Pesach is called ליל שמורים, the guarded night (Shemos 12:42), because on this night HaShem watches the life of every Jewish person. This was ordained so that the Egyptians could not claim that the 10th plague, Makas Bechoros (the Plague of the Firstborn), also afflicted the Jewish people.

In conclusion, we return to the verse ופסח ה׳ על הפתח, "and HaShem will pass over the entrance and He will not permit the Destroyer to enter your homes" (Shemos 12:23). We say on Pesach at the seder, כל שלא אמר פסח לא יצא ידי חובתו, "whoever does not tell the story of HaShem's 'passing over' the homes of בני ישראל has not fulfilled his obligation [to relate the Exodus]." The "passing over" is not an event we celebrate; it is a description of the destiny of the Jewish people. All nations eventually decay and pass away. Even the strongest and the mightiest do not last forever, for they are visited by the Mashchis. But the Mashchis passes over Israel, the eternal witness to HaShem. Because He, HaShem, is eternal, we – the witnesses – must also be eternal. It is for this reason that the haftarah for Parashas Bo concludes with Yirmiyahu's prophecy of netzach Yisrael, the eternity of Israel אתה אל תירא עבדי יעקב נאם ה כי אתך אני כי אעשה כלה בכל הגוים אשר הדחתיך שמה ואתך לא אעשה כלה ויסרתיך למשפט ונקה לא אנקיך, "you, be not afraid, my servant Yaakov – the words of HaShem – for I am with you. Though I shall make an end to all the nations where I scattered you, of you I shall not make an end" (Yirmiyahu 46:28).

Parashas Beshalach

Parashas Beshalach includes שירת הים, the Song of the Sea, which we say every day in our morning services. After HaShem had saved Israel at ים סוף, Israel responded with an outpouring of אמונה and a glorification of His name. What does the שירה come to teach us, and why was it selected by חז"ל to be recited every day?

The שירה comprises 18 psukim and was divided by the interpreters of the Torah into two sections. The first expresses glorification and praise for HaShem in His capacity as a hero-warrior who defeats the enemies of Israel. We read in שירת הים: ה' איש מלחמה, ה' שמו, "HaShem is the master of war. HaShem is His name" (Shemos 15:3). Onkelos translates this verse as "HaShem is the master of victory in war." When HaShem wills it, even a small nation can defeat larger nations. Victories such as these have occurred, viz. the Greek defeat by the Maccabees in 167 B.C.E. and, more recently, when Israel defeated four Arab armies in 1948 and 1967.

The second half of the שירה describes HaShem as a King who bestows His Land on His people. The שירה tells us, נחית בחסדך עם זו גאלת נהלת בעזך אל נוה קדשך, "With Your kindness You guided the people whom You redeemed, You led with your might to Your holy abode" (Shemos 15:13). Rashbam, Rashi's grandson, explains that when בני ישראל enter the Holy Land, ארץ ישראל will be HaShem's abode.

At the time of the crossing of ים סוף, the giving of the Torah at Har Sinai and the entrance of בני ישראל into ארץ ישראל were, of course, still in the future. It is clear that שירת הים is presenting a vision of the future in which ארץ ישראל plays a central role. However, various mefarshim, commentators on the Torah, have wondered whether שירת הים is a prayer expressing hope for the future, or whether it is a prophecy that foretells the future history of the Jewish people.

When Moshe sang שירת הים, why did he say, as the Torah

states, תבאמו ותטעמו, "You will bring them," and "You will implant them" (Shemos 15:17) instead of "bring us" and "implant us?" Rashi explains "because Moshe prophesied here that he would not enter the Land." While many commentators maintain that Moshe prayed for the future welfare of the nation – that is, that the שירה was a song of prayer – Rashi introduces the concept that Moshe sang the שירה as a song of prophecy.

The same verse in the שירה also clearly refers to ארץ ישראל and, more specifically, to Har Hamoriah: "You will bring them and implant them on the mount of Your heritage, the foundation of Your dwelling place that You, HaShem, have made; the sanctuary, my Lord, that Your hands established" (Shemos 15:17). Rashi maintains that Moshe, in the שירה, was prophesying that the Beis Hamikdash would be built, which further emphasizes that this is a prophecy and not merely a prayer.

In the last verse of שירת הים, Moshe and בני ישראל sing, ה׳ ימלך לעלם ועד, "HaShem will reign for all eternity" (Shemos 15:18). Rashi holds that "HaShem will rule forever" is a Divinely inspired declaration concerning HaShem's role until the end of time. Others might explain this pasuk as a prayer for the fulfillment of HaShem's eternal rule, but for Rashi, again, it constitutes a prophetic vision.

The Mechilta, referring to the communal experience of שירת הים, says, "a handmaid would see in a prophetic vision that which even the prophet Yechezkel ben Buzi could not see." Rav Kook, commenting on this midrash, writes that, at the time that the שירה was sung, בני ישראל collectively experienced a spiritual-prophetic uplifting to a degree never before attained. Even a person of the most modest rank, such as a handmaid, reached the level of a prophet, a navi, who spoke in the name of HaShem.

In conclusion, שירה – inadequately rendered in English as "song" – is the highest form of Divine prophecy. According to tradition, a שירה stands on a higher spiritual madregah, level, than a שיחה,

a discourse or a זימרה, a melody. A שיחה is merely an exposition of the mind on an intellectual level. It is an inner expression of the personality. On a higher level than a שיחה, is a זימרה, which is expressed from a person's neshamah, soul. It is more powerful because it is connected to the emotional expression of the person. Above both of these stands the שירה. It unites all aspects of the person with a complete expression that embraces the whole being in all of its power. We read in the Torah, כתבו לכם את השירה הזאת, "write this shirah for yourselves" (Devarim 31:19), a verse that refers to the Torah itself as shirah.

After seeing with their own eyes the great miracle of the parting of ים סוף, the Mechilta states, "great was the faith that Israel had in the One who spoke and the world came into being." The Mechilta continues, "as a reward for their faith in HaShem, there descended upon them a spirit of holiness," and they sang together שירת הים. The entire nation was uplifted to the level of singing, not a prayer of hope, but a song of Divine prophecy, sung by ordinary men and women who, at that moment, had reached a status more exalted, even, than the great prophets of Israel.

Parashas Yisro

Parashas Yisro relates the most important event in the history of the Jewish people: Matan Torah, the giving of the Torah. At Har Sinai, HaShem revealed Himself to בני ישראל and gave the 613 mitzvos, starting with the Ten Commandments. The Torah that Israel received from HaShem is not only our basic law; it is the source of our morality, our way of life and the basis for סגולת ישראל, the uniqueness of עם ישראל. Several incidents from this parashah illustrate the relationship between the Jewish people and the laws of the Torah.

The name יתרו comes from the word "yeterah," or "additional." In this instance, Yisro, Moshe's father-in-law, by his advice to Moshe, added new elements to the judicial system of Israel. He had realized that Moshe would be worn out from the need to settle disputes among the people, spending his time from morning to night judging matters large and small. Yisro therefore recommended that Moshe increase the number of judges, choosing from among the multitude אנשי חיל, יראי אלקים, אנשי אמת, שנאי בצע, "men of accomplishment, G-d-fearing men, men of truth, men who despise money" and assign them as "leaders of thousands, leaders of hundreds, leaders of fifties, and leaders of tens" (Shemos 18:21). They would adjudicate minor disputes among the people, while Moshe Rabbeinu would personally settle all major conflicts. Notice however that, according to the text, the only men Moshe was able to find were "men of accomplishment;" no mention is made of his finding "G-d-fearing men, men of truth," or "men who despise money" (Shemos 18:25).

Questions arise regarding this wise counsel from Yisro who, of course, was not an Israelite and, although he believed in the one G-d, did not join the covenant at Sinai. Do we need the wisdom of a Midianite scholar to enlighten בני ישראל on how to establish a viable system of jurisprudence? Furthermore, does this episode suggest that Moshe was not as clever as Yisro?

Rav Kook, in his book עקבי הצאן, *In the Footsteps of the Jewish People* (chapter 7), writes that universal truths that are embraced by all mankind belong to all nations. Mathematics, physics, medicine and astronomy, for instance, are common to all peoples and all cultures, and no one nation can claim them as an exclusive heritage. In the *Mishneh Torah* (Hilchos Kiddush ha-Chodesh, chapter 7), the Rambam writes that the books of the Greeks concerning astronomy, on which חז״ל based the laws regarding קידוש החודש, the sanctification of the new month, are absolutely correct. Thus, we can rely on them to fix the day of the new moon. It does not make any difference who the authors of scientific discoveries are. That is, it does not matter whether they come from among our prophets or are people of other nations. In an halachic decision, the Rambam determined that astronomy is a universal truth belonging to all mankind. Elsewhere, Rambam, himself a physician, maintained that Galenius, a Greek scholar of the second century C.E., was the father of medicine.

The idea of increasing the number of judges – of delegating judicial responsibility – cannot be attributed to any particular nation; it is a universal truth, the possession of each and every society. In addition, it is not an idea that touches the content of the law itself. It only extends the definition of those entitled to dispense justice in legal matters. It is for this reason that Moshe accepted Yisro's advice.

Another question is raised: Was Moshe not clever enough to think of the idea of increasing the number of judges and to propose it himself? Let us assume – absurdly – that Moshe Rabbeinu was not as smart as Yisro. Why would that matter? HaShem did not choose Israel because we are mankind's cleverest nation. The Midrash states, יש חכמה בגוים תאמן... יש תורה בגוים אל תאמן, "That there is wisdom in other nations, believe that; but that there is Torah in other nations, do not believe it" (Eichah Rabbah 2:13). There are nations that may possess greater talent in music, science, technology or astronomy. The Jewish people, however, were chosen to become ממלכת כהנים וגוי קדוש, "a kingdom of priests and a holy nation" (Shemos 19:6). This is the source of our uniqueness and strength; only Israel is blessed with קדושה, holiness, and only Israel possesses the unique capacity to produce נביאים, prophets. The other nations, like Israel, have the ability to participate in expanding scientific knowledge, but only Israel received the Torah.

And so we come to the Ten Commandments. The first starts with the words אנכי ה׳ אלקיך, "I am HaShem your G-d, who has taken you out of the land of Egypt from the house of slavery" (Shemos 20:2). Ibn Ezra reports that Yehuda haLevi asked him, "Why is the belief in HaShem based on the Exodus of the Jewish people from Egypt rather than on the fact that HaShem created Heaven and Earth? Is that not a greater accomplishment?" The answer is clear and simple. The Creation of Heaven and Earth, the cosmos and all that it contains, shows the absolute power and omnipotence of HaShem the Creator. However, it does not show that HaShem has a special relationship with בני ישראל, the Jewish people. When the first commandment goes on to specify אשר הוצאתיך מארץ מצרים, "who has taken you out of the land of Egypt," it confirms that HaShem continues to maintain with the Jewish people the covenant that He made with Avraham. It confirms that HaShem bestows upon the Jewish people השגחה, His Divine providence, and assures us that עם ישראל will remain עם סגולה, the Chosen People.

Parashas Mishpatim

Parashas Yisro, last week's parashah, describes the giving of the Ten Commandments. This week, Parashat Mishpatim also enumerates HaShem's laws for the Jewish people, adding a further 42 mitzvos, the majority related to civil law. Rashi declares, מה הראשונים מסיני, אף אלו מסיני, just as the former, the Ten Commandments, are מסיני (from Sinai), so the latter – dealing with matters such as liability and damages – are מסיני. Both sets of laws were given by HaShem to בני ישראל.

The Torah makes no distinction between the spiritual and ritual laws that are called מצוות בין אדם למקום, commandments between man and HaShem, and מצוות בין אדם לחבירו, commandments that concern behavior between men and their fellow men. Taken as a whole, these mandates show how all areas of life are interwoven and intertwined, and how holiness derives from honesty in business no less than from strict observance of mitzvos בין אדם למקום, between man and HaShem.

The sixth commandment, לא תרצח, do not murder, is accepted by all civilized peoples. However, for the Jewish people it is far more than an injunction against killing a human being created by HaShem. The Gemara in Bava Metzia 58b states, "He who publicly shames his neighbor it is as though he has shed blood... because ruddiness departs and paleness appears." The blood withdraws from the shamed person's face, which is also a kind of שפיכות דמים, shedding blood. One who causes humiliation בין אדם לחבירו it is as if he has taken a life. Any act that causes shame to another person, even unaccompanied by physical harm, is regarded with the utmost severity.

Similarly, the eighth commandment states לא תגנב, do not steal. This, too, is a commandment בין אדם לחבירו, between man and man, and is also much more inclusive than the usual concept of not taking money or an object that belongs to someone else. In Makkos 24a, the Gemara tells us that a buyer – a non-Jew – made an offer to Rav Safra for an item while the Rav was reciting the Shema. Rav Safra could not indicate his acceptance of the offer because it is forbidden to interrupt the recitation of the Shema. The anxious purchaser then increased his offer. When Rav Safra finally concluded his prayer he declined to accept the higher offer because, in his heart, he had decided to accept the first proposal when it was made. The Gemara explains that Rav Safra based his decision on a verse in Tehillim, ודבר אמת בלבבו, "He speaks the truth in his heart" (Tehillim 15:2). גניבת הדעת, false pretenses, is also גניבה, thievery.

In this episode, Rav Safra adhered to the principle of fulfilling the mitzvos לפנים משורת הדין, going beyond the requirements of the Torah. He showed that even in an ordinary business transaction a person can elevate himself to a higher spiritual level and draw closer to HaShem.

Yeshayahu Hanavi castigates the Jewish people for not observing the mitzvos between man and man, even as he mentions their devotion to carrying out mitzvos between man and HaShem. We read, "Why do I need your numerous sacrifices? says HaShem" (Yeshayahu 1:11), "when you spread your hands in prayer, I will hide My eyes from you; even if you were to increase prayer, I do not hear; your hands are full of blood" (Yeshayahu 1:15).

In these psukim, HaShem does not value religious behavior unaccompanied by righteous acts toward other people. HaShem refuses to accept מצוות בין אדם למקום because those who perform them are unworthy. בני ישראל is rife with people who have strayed from the mitzvos בין אדם לחבירו. The text of Yeshayahu is clear in prescribing what בני ישראל must do to have their sacrifices and prayers accepted by HaShem, "Learn to do good, seek justice, strengthen the victim, do justice for the orphan, take up the cause of the widow" (Yeshayahu 1:17). These are all mitzvos between man and his fellow man.

The chapter ends with the words ציון במשפט תפדה ושביה בצדקה, "Zion will be redeemed through justice, and those who return to her through righteousness" (Yeshayahu 1:27). Here, once again, Yeshayahu, speaking in the name of HaShem, is foretelling that the final redemption will come about through the correct loving behavior between man and man.

The Gemara, in Shabbos 31a, relates a famous story: "It happened that a certain heathen came before Hillel and said, 'Make me a convert, on condition that you teach me the whole Torah while I stand on one foot.' Hillel told him, דעליך סני לחברך לא תעביד, 'What is hateful to you, do not do to your neighbor. That is the whole of the Torah; the rest is commentary.' "

In conclusion, we must remember that ethical behavior towards our fellow men and women is absolutely essential to living a life dedicated to the mitzvos of the Torah. The civil laws of Parashas Mishpatim are מסיני no less than the Ten Commandments. Holiness and a deeper connection with HaShem derive from halachically correct business dealings no less than from strict observance of מצוות בין אדם למקום.

Parashas Terumah

In Parashas Terumah, HaShem instructs Moshe Rabbeinu to build the משכן, which is also called Ohel Moed, the Tent of Meeting, the resting place for HaShem's presence. In this parashah, the משכן is also referred to as the Mikdash, the temple that will be built in Yerushalayim.

The Rambam, in his magnum opus, the *Mishneh Torah* (Hilchos Beis Habechirah 1:1), writes that HaShem's instruction to build the משכן in the מדבר includes the mitzvah to build the Beis Hamikdash at a later time. He adds that it is a מצות עשה, a positive mitzvah, to build an abode for HaShem that will serve as the appointed place for the offering of sacrifices for the entire nation of Israel. The people are to come to Yerushalayim for the three annual pilgrimage festivals; that, explains the Rambam, is what is meant by the verse, ועשו לי מקדש ושכנתי בתוכם, "make Me a sanctuary that I may dwell among them" (Shemos 25:8). The sacrifices are to be the focal point of the mikdash, which is to serve as the meeting place of HaShem and His people.

The Rambam emphasizes that the sacrificial service will inspire the nation to strive to elevate itself spiritually to a higher level of קדושה, holiness. Yeshayahu Hanavi, for instance, was present when the sacrifices were brought to the altar to be consumed by the holy fire and was so inspired that he proclaimed קדוש קדוש קדוש ה צבאות מלא כל הארץ כבודו, "holy, holy, holy is the Lord of Hosts; the whole earth is filled with His glory" (Yeshayahu 6:3). This pasuk is the centerpiece of the Kedushah prayer that we recite several times a day.

The Ramban takes a very different approach. He does not speak of the Beis Hamikdash creating a burning desire for spiritual elevation but rather, in his introduction to Sefer Vayikra, maintains that by offering the קרבנות in the משכן, the people will merit atonement for their sins. The שכינה, the Divine Presence, would dwell in the משכן, but the attitude of בני ישראל toward the משכן and its sacrifices would be one of passive acceptance of HaShem's presence, without a striving for kedushah or a thirst for greater closeness to HaShem. As a basis for this interpretation, the Ramban quotes the very same verse as the Rambam, ועשו לי מקדש ושכנתי בתוכם, "make Me a sanctuary that I may dwell among them" (Shemos 25:8).

In a famous pasuk in Tehillim 23:6, we find what may be an example of the passivity implied by the Ramban's intepretation of the role of the mikdash. ושבתי בבית ה' לארך ימים, "and I shall dwell in the house of the Lord for many long years." In this pasuk, the psalmist exhibits no hint of personal striving for spiritual elevation, no burning aspiration to ascend to a higher degree of kedushah.

An interpretation that incorporates the approaches of both the Rambam and the Ramban can be found in *Shem MiShmuel*, an early 20th century Hasidic work. The author, Rabbi Shmuel Bornstein (1855-1927), mentions that his father, the author of *אבני נזר*, quoted the Gemara in Eruvin saying that the words מקדש and משכן are interchangeable. HaShem's dwelling place is called the מקדש, the sanctuary of the Divine, when the people come to offer up קרבנות in order to elevate themselves spiritually, as the Rambam holds. But when, as in the Ramban's approach, HaShem comes down to Earth, so to speak, then the abode of HaShem's presence is called the משכן, the Presence of the Divine.

Our relationship with HaShem can be initiated from two directions. When the initiative starts from above, when HaShem comes down to man, it is called התעוררותא דלעילא, an "awakening from above." But when the initiative starts below and is directed towards heaven, it is called התעוררותא דלתתא. In modern terms, we would say that G-d is in search of man and man is in search of G-d.

Which of these two initiatives is the more potent and the more powerful? Surely it is the latter, "man in search of G-d." To support this assertion, let us take a look at two mountains that have played important roles in Jewish history, Har Sinai and Har

HaMoriah. We read in Parashas Yisro, וירד ה' על הר סיני, "HaShem descended onto Mount Sinai" (Shemos 19:20). But after the giving of the Torah, when "HaShem comes down," Mount Sinai loses its significance forever. This was התעוררותא דלעילא. On Mount Moriah, Avraham walked for three days to reach the mountain to bring his son Yitzchak as a sacrifice to HaShem. Because of Avraham's מסירת נפש, self sacrifice, after "Avraham goes up," Mount Moriah becomes a holy mountain, the abode of HaShem, and later the site of the Beis Hamikdash. That is the potency of התעוררותא דלתתא.

According to the Rambam, HaShem commanded that the Beis Hamikdash be built because the Jewish people have always sought, and continue to seek, spiritual elevation and closeness to HaShem. In Hilchos Beis HaBechirah (6:16), the Rambam says that the שכינה is still present on the Temple Mount even though the Beis Hamikdash itself was destroyed long ago. The קדושה will remain in that place forever, just as the striving for kedushah has inspired the Jewish people from Mount Sinai to this day.

Parashas Tetzaveh / Zachor / Purim

Purim and Hannukah are דרבנן, that is to say they were instituted by חז״ל. This essay discusses how the Rishonim understood the festival of Purim and the reading of Megillas Esther. The Rambam, at the very end of Hilchos Megillah (2:18), makes a most surprising statement, "In the days of the Mashiach, all the books of the Neviim and the Kesuvim will become irrelevant, except Megillas Esther, whose status is like that of the Five Books of the Torah and the halachos of the תורה שבעל פה – the Oral Law – which will never be abolished."

This statement by the Rambam has been challenged by many of the Rishonim. The Ravad (R. Avraham Ben David, Provence, 12th century) took issue with the Rambam, writing, "Not a single book of the Tanach shall be abolished, for there is no book in which there is no Torah learning." The source of the Rambam's attitude concerning Megillas Esther is the Talmud Yerushalmi (Megillah 1:5), in which it is recorded that Rabbi Yochanan said, "the Neviim and Kesuvim shall be abolished, but the Five Books of the Torah shall not be abolished." Rabbi Shimon ben Lakish added, "Megillas Esther and the halachos shall likewise not be abolished, as it is written in the Torah, קול גדול ולא יסף, 'HaShem spoke those words with a mighty voice – those words and no more' (Devarim 5:19), and as it is written at the end of Megillas Esther, וזכרם לא יסוף מזרעם, "and the memory of them shall not perish among their descendants' (Esther 9:28)." According to this understanding, Megillas Esther is elevated to a status similar to the Five Books of Moses!

Since the Rambam's statement is based on the Yerushalmi, why did the Ravad challenge him? The fact is that the Ravad understood the sources differently. He took the term "abolish" to mean "shall cease to be read in public." With the Ravad's reading, Rabbi Yochanan was saying that the Neviim and Kesuvim shall no longer be read in public as haftaros, but Megillas Esther will continue to be read in public. He maintained, however, that the Neviim and Kesuvim will continue to be valid forever.

Even in the view of the Ravad, Megillas Esther and the Torah share a special status. As we all know, the similarity in status of Megillas Esther and the Torah extends to their physical form. In the Gemara, Rabbi Tanchum says that the Megillah must be written on ruled lines, like the Torah. It is also required to be sewn together like a sefer Torah, and it must be read like a Torah. Both the Torah and the megillah are דִּבְרֵי שָׁלוֹם וֶאֱמֶת, "words of peace and truth" (Esther 9:30), which remain valid forever.

The Rambam's halachah on Megillas Esther at the end of Hilchos Megillah (2:18) states further that "although all memory of צרות, 'misfortunes and sorrows,' will be abolished, as it is written in Yeshayahu, כִּי נשכחו הצרות הראשנות וכי נסתרו מעיני, 'The former troubles shall be forgotten and be hidden from My eyes' (Yeshayahu 65:16), the celebration of Purim shall not be abolished, as we read in Megillas Esther, וימי הפורים האלה לא יעברו מתוך היהודים וזכרם לא יסוף מזרעם, 'These days of Purim shall never cease among the Jews, and the memory of them shall never perish among their descendants' " (Esther 9:28).

This halachah is of special interest because it explains the status accorded to Purim. Midrash Mishlei states that, "the days of Purim will never be abolished." The days of Kippurim, or Yom Kippur, will also never be abolished, as it is written in Vayikra, והיתה זאת לכם לחקת עולם, 'this shall be for you a law for all time' " (Vayikra 16:34).

The source of the pairing of Purim with Yom Kippur is to be found in the *Tikkunei Zohar* (Tikkun 21). Yom Kippur is compared to Purim and, indeed, יום כפורים is stated to be the origin of the name פורים. Furthermore, in the End of Days, Yom Kippur will become a day of celebration, changing from innui (suffering) to oneg (joy). At that time, Yom Kippur will be no less a celebration than Purim. In some sources we find the comparison spelled out, Yom Kippurim k'Purim, "Yom Kippur is like Purim." But it is not of the same exalted position as Purim, which, say some sources, is even higher than that of Yom Kippur.

According to the Shelah HaKadosh (17th century Prague), on Yom Kippur we overcome our gashmius, physicality, by taking on five innuyei guf, afflictions of the body, in order to liberate ourselves from the bodily forces that subjugate us. In contrast, Purim is not a day of repression and elimination of bodily limits, but rather of the transformation of the physical into kedushah, holiness. This is the highest degree of spirituality, not כפייה, coercion, but הפיכה, transformation. Note that both words are made up of the same four Hebrew letters.

Speaking of הפיכה, the concept appears in the Megillah: ונהפוך הוא אשר ישלטו היהודים המה בשנאיהם, "On the very day that the enemies of the Jews expected to prevail over them, it was turned about; the Jews gained the upper hand over their adversaries" (Esther 9:1). The Jews not only overcame their external adversaries but also their internal adversaries; that is, the forces of physicality that prevent us from being spiritually uplifted.

The maftir for Purim speaks of our obligation to destroy Amalek. As we celebrate the victory of בני ישראל over Amalek in Persia – today's Iran – in the days of Mordechai, we must remember that at its core the essence of Purim is ונהפוך הוא, transformation (Esther 9:1). The days of fear and sorrow were transformed into days of joy that we are commanded to remember until the End of Days.

Parashas Ki Sisa

In Parashas Ki Sisa, the Torah describes in great detail the sin of the golden calf. Moshe Rabbeinu intercedes with HaShem, who graciously forgives the nation of Israel, although the actual participants are punished.

The Ten Commandments demand belief in one G-d and vehemently forbid the worship of idols, warning that the descendants of idol worshippers will be punished unto the third and fourth generations (Shemos 20:5). Two 11th century Rishonim, Rashi in France and Yehuda Halevi in Spain, offer interpretations of the text that minimize the magnitude of the transgression of the golden calf and, on this basis, explain HaShem's forgiveness.

The episode of the golden calf begins when the people demand of Aharon, "Rise up, make for us gods that will go before us" (Shemos 32:1). Rashi, in his comment on this verse, quotes the Gemara in Sanhedrin 63a, אלוהות הרבה איוו להם, "They were desirous to have many gods." Rashi indicates that בני ישראל did not deny the existence of HaShem; rather, they believed in a pantheon of gods in the world. According to this comment, the desire of בני ישראל for "many gods" did not constitute a complete denial of the first commandment, which begins with the words Anochi HaShem.

Yehuda Halevi, in his great work *The Kuzari*, addresses, among other problems, how to explain the sin of the golden calf. Rabbi Daniel Korobkin's translation of *The Kuzari* (essay 1, number 97) reads, "In those days, every people worshipped images. Even if philosophers had been able to prove to everyone the existence of the omnipotent G-d, they still would not have relinquished their images [...] The masses would not accept upon themselves any religious teaching unless it was accompanied by some image upon which they could focus their attention."

Yehuda Halevi's comment explains why Moshe Rabbeinu, when descending from Mount Sinai the first time, smashed the two tablets of the Ten Commandments. He had to destroy the image

– the tablets – that the Israelites would have wanted to worship instead of worshipping HaShem, the invisible G-d of Israel, who had taken them out of Egypt.

After the incident of the golden calf, HaShem says to Moshe, "And now desist from Me; let my anger flare up against them, and I shall annihilate them" (Shemos 32:10). This is the sort of uncompromising Divine response anticipated by the wording of the second commandment. However, Moshe successfully pleads with HaShem not to destroy Israel, although he (Moshe) takes the Jewish people to task, telling them, אתם חטאתם חטאה גדלה, "You have committed a grievous sin" (Shemos 32:30).

An explanation for HaShem's lenient treatment of בני ישראל after the incident of the golden calf can perhaps be found in the fact that the total number of people who actively participated numbered not more than 3,000 (Shemos 32:28). This is a small fraction of the masses of Israelites who took part in the sin of the מרגלים sent to spy out the Holy Land, a sin in which the whole nation participated. The Torah records, ותשא כל העדה ויתנו את קולם ויבכו העם בלילה ההוא, "The entire assembly raised up and issued its voice; the people wept that night" (Bamidbar 14:1). Furthermore, the sin committed by the מרגלים was much greater and vastly graver. HaShem could never forgive the sin of the מרגלים, spies, who rejected the Holy Land and denied HaShem in their desire to return to Egypt. Thirty thousand died then for that transgression and the rest were condemned to wander in the wilderness for 40 years. A new generation, worthy of entering the Holy Land, had to arise.

As previously mentioned in regard to Parashas Bereishis, my late father-in-law, Rav Yitzchok Amsel ז"צל, a great halachist and kabbalist, told me once that the sin of the spies was the same type of sin as that committed by Adam – an act of rebellion against HaShem. Both Adam and the מרגלים knowingly disobeyed HaShem in seeking to assume the Divine role of arbiter between good and evil. Adam was condemned to exile from גן עדן, while the nation that listened to the מרגלים had to die in the wilderness, never to enter the Holy Land. Despite appearances, these sins were far graver than the golden calf because the latter was not intended to deny malchus shamaim, the sovereignty of HaShem.

The parashah ends on a positive note. Moshe ascends Mount Sinai once more and receives a second set of tablets from HaShem. For the first time, HaShem reveals Himself as a G-d of mercy and instructs Moshe in the way that Jewish supplicants should conduct themselves when praying for forgiveness from HaShem. HaShem reveals the שלוש עשרה מדות, the thirteen attributes of Divine mercy. The prayer based on these attributes is recited on Yom Kippur and fast days, and every day in nusach Sefard. Although in the second commandment HaShem declares himself to be קל קנא פקד עון אבת על בנים, "a jealous G-d who visits the sins of the fathers on the children" (Shemos 20:5), HaShem now reveals Himself as forgiving and compassionate.

In conclusion, HaShem forgave בני ישראל for the sin of the golden calf, but punished them severely for the sin of the מרגלים. Likewise, the first Beis Hamikdash was destroyed for the sin of avodah zarah, idol worship, and בני ישראל were exiled for 70 years. However, for the sin of sinas chinam, baseless hatred, not only was the second Temple destroyed, but the Jewish people were sent into exile for 2,000 years. In our days, we are still waiting for the Geulah Shaleimah, the Final Redemption, when the third Beis Hamikdash will be built, and עם ישראל will be lovingly united – physically and spiritually – in the service of HaShem.

Parashas Vayakhel-Pekudei

The two parshiyos of Vayakhel and Pekudei record the building of the משכן and describe the bigdei kehunah, the priestly vestments. Both of these mitzvos were commanded to Moshe earlier in Shemos and our parashah records their fulfillment by Bezalel.

In Parashas Pekudei, the 39th chapter of the book of Shemos is devoted to a description of the garments worn by the High Priest. With a wealth of detail, the Torah enumerates the ornate vestments that Bezalel made for the כהן גדול to wear. After describing each item that Bezalel made, the Torah states, כאשר צוה ה את משה, "as HaShem had commanded Moshe" (Shemos 39:1, 5, 7, 21, 26, 29, 31).

As we read in Parashas Tetzaveh, HaShem first commands Moshe to make the vestments. Chapter 28 verse 2 reads, "you shall make vestments of sanctity for Aharon your brother לכבוד ולתפארת, "for splendor and beauty," or "honor and glory." In explaining the significance of the priestly vestments, most of the Torah commentators focus on this verse and, particularly, on the phrase לכבוד ולתפארת. Their explanations of that pasuk shed light on this parashah as well, where the Torah's emphasis that each garment was made exactly according to the will of HaShem shows that it was fulfilled לכבוד ולתפארת.

After reading Vayakhel and Pekudei, we may ask ourselves, is the message we are to take away that "clothes make the man?" Were the vestments for the "honor and glory" of the High Priest himself? And what kind of avodah depends for its success on outward splendor and beauty – on priestly garments, upon a breastplate with jewels, a headdress and a girdle? חז"ל have discussed these questions repeatedly over the generations and have presented original insights into the significance of the priestly vestments and, in particular, the term "honor and glory."

According to the Gemara (Zevachim 88b), the priestly vestments were intended to atone for the sins of the people. "Why are the sections [of the Torah] on the sacrifices and the priestly vestments close together? To teach you: As sacrifices make atonement, so do the priestly vestments make atonement." The Gemara then specifies the particular sins for which each part of the bigdei kehunah atoned, relying on various psukim. For instance, "the coat atones for [the sin of] bloodshed as it is said, וישחטו שעיר עזים ויטבלו את הכתנת בדם, 'And they slaughtered a he-goat and dipped the coat in the blood' (Bereishis 37:31)." Similarly, the mitznefes, headdress, atoned for arrogance, the breastplate for violations of civil law, the ephod for idolatry and the robe for lashon hara, slander.

The Rambam in his *Mishneh Torah* (Hilchos Klei Hamikdash 8:3) goes in a different direction, stating firmly that the function of the priestly vestments, like the clothes worn by a גדול, a great man, was to enhance the dignity and prestige of the wearer and his sacred office. In the eyes of the people, seeing the כהן גדול clad in beautiful, pristine garments would help inspire awe for the ceremony unfolding before them. The sacred vestments were also meant to help the priest elevate himself to the importance demanded by his office and to instil in him the confidence necessary to perform his holy task.

Many commentators stress that the sight of the כהן גדול wearing his extraordinary garments had a tremendous effect on the entire assembled community. The Yom Kippur Machzor contains a description of the כהן גדול emerging from the Holy of Holies after the Yom Kippur service. It begins, "Like the heavenly canopy stretched out over those from above, so was מראה כהן, the appearance of the כהן גדול."

This description in the Machzor is a poem with a fascinating and remarkable origin. It is based on the Book of Ben Sira. The author lived in ארץ ישראל about 200 B.C.E. He was well versed in Torah learning but also followed Hellenistic ideology. The Hebrew version of Ben Sira's book survived, and it is discussed in the Gemara. The Mishnah declares that it is not permitted to read the books of minim, heretics, but in the end the Gemara states that Ben Sira's book is not included in this category and one is allowed to read the "good things that it contains" (Sanhedrin 100b). Ben Sira's description is not based on imagination but on the real, immediate effect of seeing שמעון כהן הגדול emerge from the קודש קדושים on Yom Kippur. This is conclusive testimony of the striking effect of the "splendor and beauty" of the כהן גדול on the assembled public.

The unknown author of ספר החינך, writes that when the people saw the High Priest dressed in his beautiful vestments they would be influenced to turn their hearts to HaShem, becoming spiritually elevated when they saw the bigdei kehunah. In other words, the priest and his vestments are a means to spiritually elevate בני ישראל. According to this explanation, beauty and splendor are essential for those whose function it is to educate and to inspire.

Both interpretations hold. The priestly garb was meant both to endow sanctity and to inspire sanctity. The Gemara states that the vestments, by atoning for the sins of בני ישראל, helped restore kedushah to the entire community. By enhancing the dignity of the כהן גדול, the bigdei kehunah made it possible for him to perform his role as a sacred inspiration to the people. And by impressing the assembled congregation, the splendor of the eight specified garments helped spiritually elevate all those present and turn their hearts to HaShem.

For the reasons mentioned above, it was thus critically important for Bezalel to be meticulous in making the holy garments, as specified by the Torah for each one, כאשר צוה ה׳ את משה, "as HaShem had commanded Moshe."

3 SEFER VAYIKRA

Parashas Vayikra

Sefer Vayikra is composed almost completely of commandments, both positive and negative. Its first half is devoted to commandments relating to the משכן and to the laws of the Avodah, the Sacrificial Service. The Avodah consisted of two kinds of korbonos – animal and grain sacrifices. This essay will discuss the restoration of these two types of korbanos in the third Beis Hamikdash in Yerushalayim. We will survey the approach of our greatest Sages from the time of the Tannaim until the present.

Shortly after the destruction of the second Temple, the Tannaim determined that the Avodah will be restored when the third Temple is built in Yemos Hamashiach, the Messianic Age. This belief is reflected in the שמונה עשרה when we recite the Avodah prayer, which reads, רצה ה׳ אלקנו בעמך ישראל ובתפלתם והשב את העבודה לדביר ביתך, "Be favorable, HaShem our G-d, toward Your people Israel and their prayer, and restore the Avodah, Sacrificial Service, to Your Temple..." Then we recite, "May our eyes behold Your return to Zion in compassion. Blessed are you, HaShem, who restores His presence to Zion."

Rabbi Yehuda Halevi, who lived in Spain in the 12th century, 1,000 years after the destruction of the second Temple, supported the reinstitution of the sacrifices. He was a physician by profession and a philosopher by temperament, but the love of Zion permeated his soul. In one of his poems he wrote, "Happy are they, those who dwell in Your House; forever shall they praise You." His innermost desire was to see the restoration of the Beis HaMikdash and the Sacrificial Service in Yerushalayim.

In his poem, "O my Lord, your dwelling places are lovely," composed after he had resolved to settle in the Land of Israel, Yehuda Halevi describes a dream that transports him to the precincts of the Temple in Yerushalayim, where he sees the

Leviim occupied with the Avodah and observes the offering of sacrifices. He wakes up and, inspired, feels the sensation of HaShem hovering over him. This dream bears testimony to Yehuda Halevi's faith in the reinstatement of korbanos in the Beis HaMikdash in the End of Days. Although animal sacrifices had disappeared from the western world, Yehuda Halevi continued to believe that the mitzvah to offer korbanos in the Beis HaMikdash is one of the greatest mitzvos of the Torah.

The Rambam, Maimonides, undoubtedly the foremost halachist of all times, lived in Spain in the 12th century. On his tombstone is inscribed ממשה ועד משה לא קם כמשה, "From Moshe Rabbeinu until Moshe Maimonides, no one arose like Moshe." The very end of his *Mishneh Torah* describes the Geulah Shaleimah. It states, "Melech Mashiach will arise in the future and restore the kingship of the House of David, reestablishing its former sovereignty. He will again build the Beis Hamikdash and gather in all the dispersed of Israel. In his days all laws will be restored, and sacrifices will again be offered" (Hilchos Melachim 11:1). Yet, the Rambam acknowledges, וכל אלו הדברים וכיוצא בהן לא ידע האדם איך שיהיו עד שיהיו, "and regarding all of these matters and what arises from them, a person cannot know how it will be until it happens" (12:2).

Since the Haskalah, the so-called "Jewish Enlightenment" in the 18th and 19th centuries, there has been a reluctance to reinstitute animal sacrifices. This reluctance, as we have seen, was not shared by earlier generations and, since then, it has been actively resisted by the Torah community.

The Chafetz Chayim (1838-1933), who lived in Lithuania, was the greatest of the Gedolei Hador of his lifetime. He was the author of the *Mishnah Berurah*, widely considered to be the most authoritative codification of halachah. He believed that, in our age, we need kohanim who are fully versed in the laws of the sacrifices. Himself a kohen, he was anticipating the reestablishment of the Beis Hamikdash and the sacrifices. He therefore established a Kollel Kodshim, a special beis midrash to study the laws of Seder Kodshim in the Mishnah and the Gemara, which includes those that appear in this week's parashah. The Rambam wrote that Seder Kodshim was rarely studied in his day, but the Chafetz Chayim reintroduced the study of the laws of the sacrifices and this tradition still continues today.

However, Rav Kook, the first Chief Rabbi of Israel, believed that animal sacrifices would not be reintroduced in the third Beis Hamikdash. He brought support for his view from the words of the prophet Malachi, which are recited after every Shemoneh Esrei, וערבה לה׳ מנחת יהודה וירושלים, "Then the grain offering of Yehudah and Yerushalayim will be pleasing to HaShem as in the days of old and in previous years" (Malachi 3:4). A minchah offering is a grain offering. Given the Rambam's insistence on the lack of knowledge of the future, as mentioned above, it is possible that there may come a time when mostly grain sacrifices will be offered in the Beis Hamikdash.

In conclusion, we believe that in the third Beis Hamikdash, as the Rambam explained, animal sacrifices will continue, with the possibility that mostly grain sacrifices will eventually be offered. The question of the reinstitution of animal sacrifices is relevant in our days because we believe that we are living in the period of Aschalta D'geula, the beginning of the Final Redemption. HaShem has guided עם ישראל to return to ארץ ישראל to found a Jewish state, where the majority of the Jewish people live today. He has defended בני ישראל through nissim gedolim and He will continue to protect and maintain us there, until the coming of Mashiach and the End of Days.

Parashas Tzav / Shabbos HaGadol

The haftarah for Shabbos HaGadol is from the final chapter of the book of Malachi, the last of the Neviim – prophets. With the words, הנה אנכי שלח לכם את אליהו הנביא, "behold I send you Eliyahu the prophet" (Malachi 3:23), the authentic voice of prophecy ceased and HaShem's direct prophetic revelations to בני ישראל come to an end.

In three psukim at the end of the haftarah, in simple but expressive words, Malachi sums up the epoch of prophecy that began with Moshe Rabbeinu. He proclaims, זכרו תורת משה, "Remember the teachings of Moshe, My servant, whom I commanded חוקים and משפטים, for all Israel at Horev, i.e., Mt. Sinai" (Malachi 3:22). Mishpatim are laws whose purpose human beings can comprehend, while chukim cannot be explained through reason or human logic.

Malachi adds the spirit of Eliyahu in verse 23 to the doctrines of Moshe in verse 22. But what is the spirit of Eliyahu? He was known as a קנאי, a zealot, who declared קנא קנאתי לה׳, "I have been exceedingly zealous for HaShem" (Melachim I, 19:14), and who accused בני ישראל of breaking the Bris, the covenant, with HaShem. After being relieved of his duties as a prophet by HaShem and ascending to Heaven in a fiery chariot (Melachim II, 2:11), Eliyahu does not sever his ties to this world. Rather, a new and benevolent Eliyahu emerges. He is transformed into a protector of the Jewish people throughout the ages; a warm, beloved figure who brings hope in all generations, intervenes to help the Jewish people in times of need, and is a harbinger of good news. In the haftarah of Parashas HaGadol, we read that one of his roles is creating harmony between the generations: והשיב לב אבות על בנים ולב בנים על אבותם, "He shall restore the heart of the fathers to children and the heart of children to their fathers" (Malachi 3:24). From our own lives, we know of the tensions between generations of parents and children. Even the אבות, the forefathers of the Jewish people, suffered alienation between father and son.

An example of the "new" Eliyahu can be found in the Gemara, in the amazing story of the Tana Nachum Ish "Gam Zu," whose custom it was to respond to every occurrence by saying גם זו לטובה, "This too ("gam zu") is for the best" (Taanis 21a). Nachum was once on a mission carrying a chest full of jewels as a tribute from the Sages in ארץ ישראל to the Roman emperor. On the way, thieves stole the jewels and replaced them with dirt. Even then, Nachum said, "this too is for the best." The emperor was insulted and planned to take out his anger on Nachum and all the Sages. Thereupon, Eliyahu appeared disguised as a Roman councilor and saved the Sages and Nachum Ish Gamzu who, in the end, was sent home with great honor. In the Gemara, Eliyahu is mentioned as providing assistance to the Talmudic Sages on more than 10 occasions. The book *Tanna D'bei Eliyahu*, which was known already in Talmudic times, is attributed to him.

Eliyahu also figures in discussions of the book *Shaar HaGilgulim*, the "Gates of Reincarnation," which consist of the teachings of the Ari, Rabbi Isaac Luria (16th century), as written by his student, Rabbi Chaim Vital. It is said that the Ari heard his teachings from the mouth of Eliyahu. In the 18th century, the Baal Shem Tov said that he too had experienced גלוי אליהו, a visitation by Eliyahu.

As we all know, Eliyahu is mentioned in ברכת המזון, the Grace after Meals: "May the All-Merciful send us Eliyahu the prophet, who shall bring us good tidings, salvation and consolation." He is also present whenever a Jewish boy is circumcised; when the sandak holds the baby on his knees, the chair he sits on is known as כסא של אליהו, the Seat of Eliyahu.

On סדר night we invite Eliyahu to the festive table in several capacities. We call upon him to deliver our prayers to the Almighty. We open our doors and, in desperation, cry out: שפך חמתך על הגוים, "pour out Thy wrath upon the enemies of Israel" who arise in every generation (Yirmiyahu 10:25, quoted in the Pesach Haggadah). Towards the end of the סדר, we fill an extra cup of wine, the כוס של אליהו, which is the fifth כוס at the

סדר table. The four cups are poured to symbolize the four steps of redemption with which HaShem took בני ישראל out of Egypt. They are enumerated by the rabbis and based on psukim in the book of Shemos:

(1) והוצאתי אתכם מתחת סבלת מצרים, "I shall take you out from under the burden of Egypt,"

(2) והצלתי אתכם מעבדתם, "I shall rescue you from their service,"

(3) וגאלתי אתכם בזרוע נטויה ובשפטים גדולים, "I shall redeem you with an outstretched arm and with great judgment," and

(4) ולקחתי אתכם לי לעם והייתי לכם לאלקים, "I shall take you to Me for a people and I shall be a G-d to you" (Shemos 6:6-7).

There is a machlokhes, a debate, in the Yerushalmi (Pesachim 10:1) about whether we should drink four or five cups of wine during the סדר because of the final pasuk, והבאתי אתכם אל הארץ, I shall bring you to the Land about which I raised My hand to give it to Avraham, Yitzchak, and Yaakov" (Shemos 6:8). Like all undecided debates that cannot be resolved in the Gemara, חז"ל state, תיקו – תשבי יתרץ קושיות ובעיות, "the Tishbi, i.e., Eliyahu, will solve questions and problems." Eliyahu will reveal the explanation from within an existing law that had previously not been fully understood. But there is also a new custom in our days, among certain communities in ארץ ישראל, to drink a fifth cup because they believe that HaShem also fulfilled for them the fifth step of redemption, by bringing them into the Land.

Finally, it is important to remember that the Rambam, in the last chapter of the *Mishneh Torah*, following the spirit of Malachi, states that Eliyahu will arrive before the coming of Mashiach. The purpose of his coming is to prepare בני ישראל for the end of days and לשום שלום בעולם, to bring peace to the world. That is to say, Eliyahu is a universal personality; He is HaShem's messenger not only for בני ישראל but for the whole world!

Parashas Shemini

The tragedy of Nadav and Avihu, the two eldest sons of Aharon, is recorded in the first half of this week's parashah. They died at a moment of great joy, during the inauguration of the משכן and the installation of their father, Aharon, as כהן גדול. As Nadav and Avihu performed an unauthorized קורבן, sacrifice, in the משכן, HaShem sent down a fire that consumed them. What was the nature of their sin? The Torah tells us, ויקריבו לפני ה' אש זרה, "and they brought before HaShem a strange fire that He had not commanded them to do" (Vayikra 10:1).

The severity of the Divine act of retribution has puzzled all who study the Torah. It would appear that the sin of Nadav and Avihu was much greater than a superficial reading might suggest. In every generation, new insights and explanations have been proposed to explain the magnitude of their transgression.

Although the Torah clearly states that "they brought before HaShem a strange fire that He had not commanded them to do," the Midrash (Vayikra Rabbah 20:8) provides further explanation and interpretation, citing four grave sins committed by Aharon's two oldest sons:

(1) They entered the קודש קדושים, the holiest part of the משכן.

(2) They offered a sacrifice that HaShem had not commanded.

(3) They did not bring the fire from a holy source.

(4) They did not consult with each other beforehand.

The Gemara in Eruvin 63a proposes two additional sins, namely that Nadav and Avihu had decided a halachah in the presence of Moshe Rabbeinu. This was an unforgivable act of rebellion. In addition, they had drunk too much wine before the sacrificial service, which – as recorded later in the parashah (Vayikra 10:9) – is strictly forbidden.

The Gemara continues by stating that when Nadav and Avihu followed Moshe and Aharon in the procession, Nadav said to Avihu, "Before long, these two old men will be gone, and we will be the leaders of the community." According to this view, they did not violate a specific commandment but rather showed profound disrespect for Moshe Rabbeinu. They entertained unfilial designs, exhibited unscrupulous ambition and acted out of envy for those in high positions. The rabbis of the Middle Ages found fault with Nadav and Avihu, not only for committing specific sins, but also for their מדות רעות, their bad character traits.

However, the text of the parashah suggests a totally different explanation. We read that when Moshe consoled Aharon upon the death of his two sons, Moshe said to him, "Of this HaShem speaks, saying, בקרבי אקדש, "I will be sanctified through those who are nearest to Me" (Vayikra 10:3). Here we see that, after their deaths, Nadav and Avihu were sanctified as צדיקים. In a similar vein, the Sifra explains Nadav and Avihu's offence by stating, "They too, in their joy, as soon as they saw the new fire, stood forth to heap אהבה על אהבה, love unto their love. 'And each one took his fire pan' " (Vayikra 10:1). Their guilt was not the result of a formal transgression of any of the laws involved in the sacrificial service, but rather lay in their desire to break through, as it were, to HaShem, to cleave to Him – not in conformity with the mitzvos of the Avodah, but rather according to the dictates of their hearts. The acceptance of the Yoke of Heaven, which is the aim of the Torah, is here replaced by a religious ecstasy that is free from the frame of normative religious discipline. Their act was לשמה ולא כהלכה for the sake of Heaven but not as commanded by HaShem. They were צדיקים, but for this sin they were punished.

Rabbi Samson Rafael Hirsch (1808-1888), the founder of *Torah im Derech Eretz*, in his work *Horeb*, states, "Closeness and nearness to HaShem can only be attained by being disciplined to His will – this is the chasm separating Judaism from idolatry. The idolater wishes to bend his god to his own will and heart's desire by means of the sacrifice, whilst the Jew wishes, through his sacrifice, to stimulate himself to fulfill the will of the Creator." He concludes, "Only by observance of the precepts of the Torah can a Jewish person remain true to his principles."

Nadav and Avihu, although their intention to draw close to HaShem was pure, got "carried away" and lost the discipline and focus necessary to perform the mitzvos of the Avodah.

The Rambam, in the *Mishneh Torah* (Hilchos Me'ilah 8), differentiates between two kinds of mitzvos: mishpatim, laws, and chukim, statutes. The reason for the former, such as the prohibitions against theft and murder, can easily be grasped by the human mind, while the reasons for the latter, for example kosher food, cannot. Both must be followed with equal fidelity and stringency for it is by carrying out the mitzvos, whether we understand them or not, that the righteous will earn a place in the World to Come. Although the korbanos, sacrifices, are among those mitzvos whose reasons are unclear to us, writes the Rambam, "our Sages said that it is for the sacrifices that the world exists" (Hilchos Me'ilah 8:8).

Some commentators see specific transgressions as the cause of Nadav and Avihu's severe punishment, while others state that they "followed the dictates of their heart" rather than cleaving to the discipline of the mitzvos. What is clear is that they strayed from the laws set down by HaShem, giving their own deviant interpretation for the Avodah. By trying to "improve on" what HaShem commanded, they introduced an אש זרה, strange fire, into the משכן.

Rabbi Shlomo Aviner, the Rosh Yeshivah of Yeshivas Ateres Kohanim, presents a mystical interpretation in his book טל חרמון. He quotes The Kuzari of Rav Yehudah HaLevi in stating that the function of the Beis Hamikdash is to unite the fire from this world with the fire from the upper world. Thus, the united fire, in its totality, is enveloped in the upper world. That is what the Gemara means in Yoma 21b when it states, אף על פי שאש יורדת מן השמים מצוה להביא מן ההדיוט, "even though the fire descends from heaven, it is a mitzvah to light [a fire] from the profane." If one performs the Avodah in the Beis Hamikdash in the correct state of mind, with a pure heart, then Earth and Heaven will be connected.

Parashas Tazria-Metzora

The haftarah for Parashas Metzora is from Melachim II, chapter 7, and tells the story of four metzoraim, people stricken with leprosy. The Gemara (Sotah 47) tells us that the four metzoraim are Gechazi and his three sons. Earlier, in the haftarah of Tazria, they had been cursed with leprosy by the prophet Elisha (Melachim II 5:27) for soliciting clothing and money from Naaman, the military commander of the king of Aram. Later, when the city of Shomron, the capital of the Northern Kingdom, was near starvation because of a siege by the Arameans, the lepers brought to בני ישראל the good news that the Aramean army had fled and left behind plentiful supplies.

Rabbi Yitzchak Eizik HaLevi Rabinowitz (1847-1914) was an outstanding talmid chacham in the yeshiva of Volozhin and a historian who took issue with the interpretations of Jewish history proposed by the Maskilim, proponents of the Jewish Enlightenment. He is best known as the author of *Doros HaRishonim*, a multi-volume work on the history of the religious life of ancient Israel. He writes that in the period of the Shoftim – the Judges – בני ישראל lived a fully religious life of Torah and mitzvos, according to traditions passed down from their forefathers who had stood at Sinai.

The haftarah of Parashas Metzora provides an interesting illustration of the halachos that were observed in the periods of the Shoftim. These halachos were only much later codified in the Mishnah. Gechazi is one of the people about whom the rabbis of the Mishnah say, אין לו חלק לעולם הבא, "He does not have a share in the world to come" (Sanhedrin 10:2). Yet it is clear from the text of the haftarah that he and his three sons accepted completely the laws of the Torah concerning metzoraim. That is, they lived in total isolation from the rest of the community. After all, it was from outside the city gate that Gechazi and his sons set out to find food and happened upon the deserted Aramean encampment.

According to Rav Eizik HaLevi, another example of mitzvos known to us from the Mishnah being followed in this period is to be found in the book of Shmuel I. Specifically, when Shabbos falls on Erev Rosh Chodesh, we recite a haftarah that begins with the words: "Yonasan said to David, 'machar chodesh – tomorrow is the new moon – and you will be missed because your seat will be empty.'" (1 Samuel 20:18).

A few psukim later we read, "During the New Moon... the king (Shaul) sat down to eat as usual... but David's seat was empty. Shaul said nothing that day, for he thought מקרה הוא בלתי טהור הוא כי לא טהור, 'something has happened (mikrah). He (David) must be impure, for he has not been cleansed.'" (1 Samuel 20:24-26). "It was the day after Rosh Chodesh, i.e., the second day of Rosh Chodesh, and David's place was empty. Shaul said to Yonasan, his son, 'Why did the son of Yishai not come to the seudah yesterday or today?' " (1 Samuel 20:27).

The details of this incident demonstrate that Shaul – and everyone else concerned – was conversant with the laws of tumah and taharah. They knew that a baal keri remains tamei until nightfall, when he has to immerse himself in a mikveh. They also knew that a rishon letumah cannot make another person tamei but is considered tamei if he goes to a holy place. In addition, a rishon letumah can render ochlin – food – tamei, so David could have attended the seudah but would have been unable to partake of the meal. He thus applied the laws of Mishnah Zavim (5:11), which were instituted about 1,200 years later.

From this haftarah we also see that, in the days of Shaul, the people observed two days of Rosh Chodesh. They knew that Rosh Chodesh could fall only on the 30th or 31st day after the previous Rosh Chodesh. Therefore, Yonasan said to David, "machar chodesh," tomorrow will be Rosh Chodesh, and Shaul asked Yonasan, "Why did David not come either yesterday or today?" These conversations show that two days of Rosh Chodesh, which are not mentioned in the Torah, were being observed according to rules formalized into halachah only in the time of the Tannaim.

It is worth noting that Shaul and his court were already celebrating the new month with a seudas Rosh Chodesh. So we see that in our days, when we celebrate the new month with a meal, we are following a beautiful tradition already practiced in the time of Shaul.

Finally, let us take a look at the Book of Ruth, which we read on Shavuos and which is most eloquent in describing day-to-day life in the time of the Judges. It is interesting to note that, in that era, the common people observed two halachic practices that were codified only many generations later. For example, Naomi tells Ruth, "It is best, daughter, that you go out with his [Boaz's] young women, rather than with his male workers" (Ruth 2:21). We see here that even in this early period, tzniyus, modesty, although not detailed as a mitzvah in the Torah, was considered most important.

Also in Megillas Ruth, we find the passage, "To validate any transaction, one man would take off his sandal and hand it to the other" (Ruth 4:7). The exchange of a shoe established that a transaction had been concluded. Although the halachic laws of kinyan, validation of a transaction, were only established in the time of the Amoraim, we see that בני ישראל lived according to these practices centuries before the תורה שבעל פה was written down.

From these examples it is clear that, as Rabbi Yitzchak Eizik HaLevi Rabinowitz maintained, the mitzvos of the Torah and, to a certain extent, the תורה שבעל פה were already being observed by בני ישראל in the time of the Shoftim. This confirms that the תורה שבעל פה was given at Mt. Sinai together with the תורה שבכתב.

Parashas Acharei-Kedoshim

This remarkable parashah occupies the midpoint of Sefer Vayikra, the middle book of the Torah, but it owes its central position in our tradition to much more than its location in the Chumash. The Midrash tells us that רוב גופי התורה, the essentials of the Torah, are summarized in Parashas Kedoshim (Rashi on Vayikra 19:2); it is in the center, because it is central!

Our parashah begins, "Speak to the entire assembly of the children of Israel and say to them, קדשים תהיו כי קדוש אני ה' אלוקיכם, 'You shall be holy for holy am I, Your G-d' " (Vayikra 19:2). HaShem says "holy am I" because He is the source of kedushah, sanctity. חז"ל refer to HaShem as HaKadosh Baruch Hu, "The Holy One, Blessed Be He."

Many people have the impression that sanctity can be found only outside of everyday life, in the lives of tzaddikim, perhaps, or in the Messianic Age. The Torah, however, tells us, ואתם הדבקים בה' אלקיכם חיים כלכם חיום, "But you who cling to HaShem your G-d are alive today" (Devarim 4:4). In other words, we are alive because we cling to the source of kedushah, HaShem, by fulfilling the mitzvah of קדושים תהיו, that is, by striving to extend and fully develop our kedushah. קדושים תהיו is a mitzvah and a havtachah; it is both a commandment and a promise.

The word "holy" can apply to time, place and people. In the story of Creation, we find the kedushah of Shabbos, ויברך אלקים את יום השביעי ויקדש אתו, "HaShem blessed the seventh day and sanctified it" (Bereishis 2:3). It is a holy time. We also find holiness in specific places. The first location described by the Torah as admas kodesh, holy ground, is the area around the sneh – the Burning Bush – where Moshe was commanded to remove his shoes (Shemos 3:5). In addition, the Rambam (Hilchos Beis HaBechirah, chapter 6) states that ארץ ישראל and specifically Har Habayis, the Temple Mount, are sanctified with the presence of the Shechinah for all time.

Finally, people can be holy. At Ma'amad Har Sinai – when He gave the Torah, HaShem commanded בני ישראל to be a ממלכת כהנים וגוי קדוש, "a kingdom of kohanim and a holy nation" (Shemos 19:6). The holiness of עם ישראל is confirmed in Devarim, עם קדוש אתה לה' אלקיך, "you are a holy people to HaShem, your G-d" (Devarim 7:6). Every Jewish person possesses innate sanctity because of the holy soul of עם ישראל.

The Rambam says at the end of Hilchot Shemitah that kedushah is not limited to the tribe of Levi; all of Israel can be kadosh if they strive to serve HaShem. However, there are different madregos, levels, of saintliness. In the long history of the Jewish people, only five Sages are considered to have reached the highest level of kedushah. They are Rabbeinu Hakadosh (Yehudah HaNasi, 2nd century C.E., the author of the *Mishnah*); the Ari Hakadosh (16th century, the great kabbalist whose work was transcribed by Rav Chaim Vital in the book *Etz Chayim*); the Alshich Hakadosh (16th century, author of *Toras Moshe*, a commentary on the Torah); the Shelah Hakadosh (17th century, the writer of *Shnei Luchos Habris* and the founder of the Horowitz families); and finally, the Ohr Hachaim Hakadosh (18th century, Morocco, the author of the *Ohr Hachaim* commentary on the Torah).

However, the Rambam did not include "striving for holiness" in his list of the 613 mitzvos of the Torah. In *Sefer HaMitzvos* (chapter 4), he declared that קדושים תהיו – "be holy" – cannot be considered a separate and independent action that every Jew must proactively perform. Rather, it is only a mitzvah koleles, a general commandment. Only if a Jew performs the Torah's clearly defined positive and negative mitzvos can he hope to achieve kedushah, holiness. This is why every time we recite a brachah, a blessing, we praise HaShem, אשר קדשנו במצוותיו, "who sanctified us with His commandments." Performing the mitzvos is a sanctification; the person who carries them out is elevated and attains kedushah.

Holiness is a feature of the everyday lives of men and women. The words, "You shall be holy", must be understood as commanding the performance of the precepts spelled out in this week's parashah. This includes reverence for parents, consideration of the needy, prompt payment of wages, dealing honorably with all men, avoiding tale-bearing or malice, showing cordiality to the foreigner, implementing equal justice for both rich and poor, and using just measures and balances. This list of commandments concludes with the words, ואהבת לרעך כמוך, "love thy neighbor as thyself" (Vayikra 19:18). It is by fulfilling the commandments of the parashah that a Jewish person can live a life of true kedushah.

The Ramban (1194-1270) was the greatest talmudist after the Rambam and the leading figure among the kabbalists of Gerona in Catalonia. In a most insightful comment on קדושים תהיו, he admonishes us that our behavior, if it is to lead to kedushah, must be governed by moderation, even when we perform acts that are permitted. The Torah allows the eating of certain meats and the drinking of wine at special occasions, and obligates conjugal relations between husband and wife at the proper time. While remaining technically within the law, a man with unbridled desires could become a gluttonous eater of meat, a wine-drinker and lustful in his relations with his wife. He could, in the words of the Ramban, become a נבל ברשות התורה, "a degenerate person within the permitted realm of the Torah." To prevent such a possibility, the Ramban stated a guiding character principle, קדש עצמך במותר לך – "Sanctify yourself" – through moderation and sobriety – "even in matters that are permitted."

In conclusion, "striving for sanctity" may not be one of the 613 mitzvos of the Torah – on this point the Ramban agrees with the Rambam – but it constitutes the spirit in which the mitzvos must be performed if we are to achieve kedushah.

Parashas Emor

In Parashas Emor, the Torah enumerates the chagim, the festivals of the Jewish people. We read, אלה מועדי ה' מקראי קודש אשר תקראו אתם במועדם, "These are the appointed festivals of HaShem, the holy convocations, which you shall designate in their appropriate time" (Vayikra 23:4). The festivals are also mentioned in four other parshiyos: Mishpatim, Ki Sisa, Pinchas and Re'eh, but according to the *Midrash* (Sifre on Devarim 16:1), the festival cycle presented in Parashas Emor is the most comprehensive.

The chagim are described in connection to agricultural times but are also associated with historical events. Pesach, of course, is connected historically with Yetzias Mitzraim, the Exodus from Egypt, and for this reason requires the performance of mitzvos such as the eating of matzah. In Parashas Emor, Sukkos and the mitzvah of building a sukkah are also given a historical context: "You shall dwell in booths for a seven-day period, and every native in Israel shall dwell in booths, so that your generation will know that I caused the children of Israel to dwell in them when I took you out of the land of Egypt" (Vayikra 23:42-43).

It is therefore quite extraordinary that the historical significance of Shavuos is not mentioned in the parashah or, for that matter, anywhere else in the Torah. Furthermore, no symbols or acts – similar to the lulav on Sukkos for example – are associated with this holiday. On Shavuos we celebrate HaShem's revelation on Mount Sinai and the giving of the Torah. In the text of our prayers, Shavuos is referred to as זמן מתן תורתנו, "the season of the giving of the Torah," and for this reason the Torah reading on Shavuos retells the central event in our history, the giving of the Ten Commandments (Shemos 20). Why, then, does the parashah not state that on this day we are to remember that HaShem gave the Torah to His nation? This question is asked by Rabbi Yitzchak Arama (Spain, 1420-1494) in his book עקידת יצחק. Rabbi David Tzvi Hoffmann (Germany, 1843-1921) poses another interesting question, one hinted at a moment ago: Why does Shavuos lack a symbol?

Rav Arama answers both questions, stating that the acquisition of the Torah is a timeless mitzvah; it must not be seen as a one-time event, as were the Exodus from Egypt and the splitting of the Red Sea. Matan Torah is an ongoing process that continues throughout all generations. In Devarim, we read, היום הזה ה׳ אלקיך מצוך לעשות את החקים האלה, "This day HaShem your G-d commands you to perform these decrees" (Devarim 26:16). Rashi cites the Midrash on this verse, "every day it should be as if commanded today." We also are mindful of what HaShem said to Yehoshua, "The Book of the Torah will not depart from your mouth, but you shall meditate therein by day and by night" (Yehoshua 1:8). When we celebrate the giving of the Torah, we do not commemorate a one-day event that took place at Har Sinai but rather recognize that the process of understanding the Torah and living by it requires continual engagement. Every moment of Torah study reminds us of the Torah's Divine source. It is for this reason that the conclusion of Birkas Hatorah, the blessings over the Torah, is formulated in the present tense נותן התרה, "He who gives the Torah," and not in the past tense נתן התורה, "who gave the Torah." Every day we continue the process of acquiring the Torah.

On the topic of Shavuos, there is a phrase in the parashah that has engendered a great deal of controversy but is the key to celebrating Shavuos on the right day: וספרתם לכם ממחרת השבת, "You shall count for yourselves, from the morrow of Shabbos... seven complete weeks" (Vayikra 23:15). The reference, of course, is to the counting of the omer, which determines the date of Shavuos. [What is the omer? An omer is a measure of dry matter. It is also the amount of flour that had to be brought to the Beis Hamikdash as an offering on the second day of Pesach. The offering, and thus the counting whose beginning it marked, came to be known as the omer.]

חז״ל explained (Menachos 65b) that the word שבת in the pasuk just quoted should not be understood as meaning that the days of the omer are to be counted from the day after the Shabbos of Pesach. Rather, the counting must begin on the day after the first day of yom tov of Pesach, which is not the seventh day of the week but is considered a day of rest, which is a kind of שבת. The second day of Pesach is thus the first day of the omer.

At the time of Bayis Sheni, a sect known as the צדוקים, the Sadducees, was very powerful politically and religiously, so much so that they controlled the Beis Hamikdash. They refused to accept the legitimacy of the תורה שבעל פה, the Oral Law, and they insisted that the 49 days of the omer should begin on the day after the Shabbos following the Pesach seder. As a result, Shavuos would always fall on the first day of the week. They wanted Shavuos to be a secular agricultural festival without HaShem or Torah. The Sadduccees ceased to exist after the destruction of the second Beis Hamikdash. Of course, the halachah follows חז״ל that ממחרת השבת indicates the second day of Pesach.

In conclusion, this parashah teaches us that the Jewish people can only exist with absolute belief in HaShem, the Torah and the teachings of חז״ל. The chagim and their strict observance confirm that belief.

Parashas Behar-Bechukosai

Parashas Bechukosai starts with the benedictions that await the Jewish people if they live up to their covenant with HaShem. It then proceeds to the תוכחה, the admonition, a sobering account of the punishments that will befall the holy nation if its people do not heed the words of HaShem and fulfill the commandments.

The Torah describes two sets of admonitions, one in this week's parashah and the other in Parashas Ki Savo, toward the end of Sefer Devarim. These two sets of תוכחת are not identical. The one in Ki Savo does not offer the hope that the Jewish people will be able to avert the foretold disasters. The tone of the תוכחה in Bechukosai, however, is very different. Here, HaShem's warnings are tempered with compassion. HaShem promises that He will not abandon His nation or the national homeland, ארץ ישראל. We read in the parashah, וזכרתי את בריתי יעקב ואף את בריתי יצחק ואף את בריתי אברהם אזכר והארץ אזכר, "I will remember my covenant with Yaakov, and also my covenant with Yitzchak, and also my covenant with Avraham, and I will remember the Land" (Vayikra 26:42).

The following discussion of the parashah draws on the interpretations of the Ramban, who lived in Spain in the 13th century and was also one of the leading kabbalists of his age. It also relates to the views of Abarbanel, an advisor to the kings of 15th century Portugal and Spain, who is also well known as a commentator on the Tanach.

The Ramban believed that the תוכחה in Parashas Bechukosai applied to the period of Bayis Rishon, which was destroyed by Nebuchadnezzar, king of Babylon, in 586 B.C.E. The Jewish people had succumbed to idol worship and, as punishment, were taken into exile in Babylon for 70 years, a period that reflects the length of time during which they failed to observe the שמיטה, the sabbatical year, in ארץ ישראל. As we read in the parashah, אז תרצה הארץ את שבתתיה כל ימי השמה, "then the Land will be appeased for its sabbaticals during all the years of its desolation" (Vayikra 26:34). It is clear from this pasuk that the text refers specifically to the period of Bayis Rishon.

The Ramban further maintains that the other תוכחה, in Parashas Ki Savo, applies to the period of Bayis Sheni, which culminated in the destruction of the Beis Hamikdash in 70 C.E. by the Romans under Titus. The Ramban supports this interpretation by quoting from Ki Savo: ישא ה' עליך גוי מרחק מקצה הארץ כאשר ידאה הנשר גוי אשר לא תשמע לשנו, "HaShem will carry against you a nation from afar, from the end of the earth, as an eagle will swoop, a nation whose language you will not understand" (Devarim 28:49). During the period of Bayis Sheni, the Jews of ארץ ישראל did not understand Latin, the language of the Romans. Furthermore, the eagle was the symbol of Rome. During the period of Bayis Rishon, on the other hand, they did understand Aramaic, the language of Babylon. The admonition in Ki Savo must therefore refer to the period of Bayis Sheni.

The Ramban believed that exile, such as the Babylonian captivity, and redemption, such as the return of the exiles from Babylon, should not be seen as one-time events in Jewish history. Rather, exile and redemption take place again and again, and will continue to recur until the final redemption in the Messianic Age.

The view of Abarbanel is totally different. He challenges the interpretation of the Ramban, asserting that there was only one true חורבן – the destruction of the first Beis Hamikdash. According to his view, all subsequent exiles suffered by the Jewish nation were the result of this singular catastrophe. Abarbanel argues that the תוכחה in this parashah is addressed both to those exiled to Babylon and to those forced to leave ארץ ישראל by the destruction of the second Beis Hamikdash. Similarly, the תוכחה in Ki Savo refers to the exilic periods that followed the destruction of both Batei Hamikdash.

Abarbanel holds that there is only one redemption, the final and full redemption at the End of Days, of which the prophets of Israel speak so eloquently. Abarbanel disagrees further with the

Ramban's interpretation of this parashah, saying instead that the destruction of Bayis Rishon was not followed by a גאולה. Although King Cyrus of Persia gave permission to the returnees from exile in Babylon to rebuild the Beis Hamikdash in Yerushalayim, he never ceded his rights as the sovereign ruler of the Land of Israel. Furthermore, argues Abarbanel, there was no kibbutz galuyos, ingathering of exiles, when the Babylonian captives returned to ארץ ישראל after 70 years. Only 42,360 men returned, whereas the vast majority of Jews remained in Bavel. Can this be called redemption? Rather, it was a פקידה, a Divine remembrance, a period of relative comfort and rest from war.

Towards the end of his life, Abarbanel settled in Italy, forced by the Inquisition to leave the Iberian Peninsula. The Ramban also had to leave Spain following a religious disputation held in the presence of the king, but he went to ארץ ישראל. The Babylonian captivity ended with the return to the Land of Israel of a small number of Jews, a mini-redemption that, as the Ramban saw, was followed by another exile. The aliyos of our era, however, have brought a majority of Jews to the Land of Israel. We hope and pray that this is ראשית צמיחת גאולתנו, the beginning of the Flowering of our Redemption!

4 SEFER BAMIDBAR

Parashas Bamidbar

This week, we begin the fourth book of the Torah, Bamidbar, offering us an opportunity to discuss this sefer in the context of חמישה חומשי התורה, the Five Books of Moshe. In the Middle Ages the Rishonim, especially Ramban and Abarbanel, wrote extensively about the distinctness and purpose of each of the five books of the Torah.

Concerning the first book of the Torah, Bereishis, Abarbanel writes that it is to be considered a book of genealogy, since it describes the descent of all mankind from Adam, the first human being created by HaShem. While that is true, given the many geneologies in the book, Rashi famously comments on the first verse of the Torah, asking why it was necessary to start the Torah with the words, בראשית ברא אלקים. Rather, he states, it could have begun with the first mitzvah ever commanded to בני ישראל in Sefer Shemos, "This month shall be for you the beginning of the months, it shall be for you the first of the months of the year" (Shemos 12:1). In that way, the Torah would have started with the emergence of the Nation of Israel during the Exodus from Egypt. The Book of Bereishis is part of the Torah but serves as an introduction for the other four books. This shows the importance of מעשה בראשית, Creation, in HaShem's scheme.

The second book of the Torah, Shemos, introduces the role of עם ישראל as HaShem's chosen nation. The climax of Shemos, indeed of the entire Torah, takes place after the Exodus from Egypt at Mount Sinai, where HaShem chooses the Jewish people as His own and gives them the Ten Commandments. This event was, without doubt, the greatest moment in Jewish history.

Shemos also introduces the concept of kedushah, the source of which is HaShem. Only the people of Israel are possessed of kedushah, which makes it possible for them to be HaShem's chosen nation and for HaShem to dwell among them. In fact,

HaShem commanded them, ‏ואתם תהיו לי ממלכת כהנים וגוי קדוש‎, "you shall be to Me a kingdom of priests and a holy nation" (Shemos 19:6). Abarbanel comments that the unique sanctity of ‏בני ישראל‎ was inherited from the ‏אבות‎, the forefathers of the nation.

Shemos concludes with detailed instructions for the building of the ‏משכן‎, the holy abode of HaShem among ‏בני ישראל‎. The ‏משכן‎ was to be the focal point of the Jewish people's encampment in the ‏מדבר‎. The most profound message of Shemos is that HaShem seeks to dwell among the Jewish people forever.

Whereas Shemos introduces the concept of kedushah, all of the commentators, without exception, agree that Vayikra is the book of holiness, putting the idea of kedushah into practice. This unique sefer sets forth the laws and commandments concerning the Avodah, the Sacrificial Service in the ‏משכן‎. HaShem can only reside in the midst of a nation that maintains kedushah. Vayikra establishes for the Kohanim, or priests, as well as the Levites and the ordinary people, the many mitzvos necessary for a holy life. Vayikra is thus often referred to as Sefer Kedushah, the Book of Sanctity. These commandments and laws must be adhered to by all of Israel for all generations. That is why blessings over mitzvos include the words, ‏אשר קדשנו‎ ‏במצותיו וציונו‎, "Who sanctified us with His mitzvos, which He commanded us." In Eastern Europe, before the Second World War, boys as young as three or four years old started in cheder, religious school, with the book of Vayikra. They were lovingly called the ‏צאן קודשים‎ – the holy sheep.

The fourth sefer, Bamidbar, records the struggles of ‏בני ישראל‎ while they lived in the wilderness according to the mitzvos given at Sinai. More than half of Sefer Bamidbar deals with the failings of the generation that left Egypt: they craved meat, dreamt nostalgically about their lives as slaves, and rejected the sovereignty of HaShem and His mitzvos. The second part of Bamidbar, which covers the people's 40th year in the ‏מדבר‎, portrays the Israelites preparing to enter the Land of Israel. The wanderings of בני ישראל in the מדבר for 40 years were ordained because of the sin of the meraglim, the spies. The generation that left Egypt was born into slavery and needed a period in the מדבר in order to develop a consciousness of sanctity and spirituality. The Book of Bamidbar conveys an interesting diversity of commandments. In his commentary, Ramban struggles to define their character. He comments that many of the mitzvos are temporary and only applied to בני ישראל during their sojourn in the wilderness (Ramban's commentary on Bamidbar 1).

The Book of Devarim is the concluding book of the Torah. On the last day of his life, Moshe instructs the Israelite nation, repeating the mitzvos and advising them of their future destiny. After 40 years in the wilderness, בני ישראל were ready to observe all of the mitzvos necessary for HaShem to maintain His Presence in their midst, and to enter the Land.

In conclusion, note that the Torah states in Devarim, בנים אתם לה׳ אלקיכם. בני ישראל are the children of HaShem (Devarim 14:1). However, the Zohar goes further and explains in Parashas Vayikra, קודשא בריך הוא, ישראל, ואורייתא חד הוא, "the Holy One Blessed Be He, the Torah, and Israel are one" (Parashas Vayikra 73). עם ישראל and the Torah are inseparably connected to HaShem for all time.

Parashas Naso

The themes of Parashas Naso are varied. However, all of its topics have a common denominator, namely, that they are in some way related to the Beis Hamikdash. This essay focuses on the laws of the נזיר, the Nazirite. Furthermore, we will explore how the perception of the nazir changed over time.

What is the meaning of the word נזיר? In the book of Bereishis, Yaakov, in his blessing to Yosef, calls him נזיר אחיו (Bereishis 49:26). The Targum Onkelos translates it as "separate from his brothers." A נזיר is a person who wishes to live a higher and more spiritual life than does the ordinary Jewish person. In fact, we read that the laws of spiritual purity that apply to the נזיר are the same as those of the כהן גדול, the High Priest, who is not permitted to make himself tamei – impure, in any way, even upon the death of his father or mother.

The parashah explains the laws of the נזיר but, in the entire Tanach, there are only two explicit cases of נזירים, Shimshon and Shmuel, both at the time of the Shoftim, or Judges. In this period, avodah zarah was very prevalent, to the extent that children were sacrificed and burnt in fire to the Canaanite avodah zarah of Moloch. Perhaps this is why בני ישראל needed נזירים to elevate them and counter the avodah zarah. It is worth noting that the mothers of both Shmuel and Shimshon dedicated their sons to נזירות before they were born, unlike the laws in the parashah where an adult takes the vow. In halachah, such a "pre-natal" נזיר is called Nezirus Shimshon.

When Shmuel takes on the role of navi, the institution of the נזיר disappears, which implies that it is no longer desirable. Yet, a study of the works of the great prophets Amos and Yirmiyahu reveals a great appreciation of נזירות. Amos states, ואקים מבניכם לנביאים ומבחוריכם לנזירים, "And I raised up from among your sons for prophets and from among your young men for Nazirites" (Amos 2:11).

However, by the time of the Tannaim, the neder, or vow, of the

נזיר was considered to be of debatable merit. Indeed, in our parashah, it is explicit that the נזיר was required to bring a sin offering to the Beis Hamikdash as atonement for having חטא על הנפש, "sinned on the soul" (Bamidbar 6:11). What is the sin of the נזיר? The Gemara in Taanis 11a brings two opposing views. Shmuel states that fasting for self-affliction is considered a sin. He is supported by Rabbi Elazar HaKappar, who declares that the sin of the נזיר is specifically of depriving himself of wine. The opposing view is taken by Rabbi Elazar. He believes that the נזיר is a kadosh, a holy person, as it is written in the parashah (Bamidbar 6:5), קדוש יהיה גדל שער פרע ראשו, "he shall be holy to HaShem, the hair on his head shall grow wild."

Two of the greatest Rishonim, the Rambam and the Ramban, each adopted one of the opinions expressed in the above-mentioned Talmudic debate. The Rambam sided with the view of Rabbi Elazar HaKappar, while the Ramban sided with Rabbi Elazar.

The Rambam interprets the Torah in his *Shmonah Perakim*, writing that the נזיר should be considered a sinner. In taking additional stringencies upon himself, the נזיר breaks the Rambam's golden rule, which is that one should follow the middle road of moderation. That is, one should eat and drink in moderation, live within the community, and refrain from afflicting one's body. In short, one should do nothing in excess, a concept that the נזיר, by definition, violates.

In a similar vein, in Hilchos Nezirus, the Rambam writes that a person is forbidden to mortify his body. He should wear regular clothes, not sackcloth, which was the cloth of monks. He may only deny himself that which the Torah forbids him. Thus, the Rambam gives his complete support to the opinion of Rabbi Elazar HaKappar, that the נזיר is a sinner.

The Ramban, on the other hand, writes that the נזיר "sins against his soul" only when he forsakes his vows of abstinence, that is, when his days of being a נזיר have been fulfilled. In other words, once the נזיר has taken upon himself to be holy unto

HaShem by adhering to the strictures of נזירות, he should continue to live a life of holiness and of separateness from the rest of the community. The Ramban considers the נזיר to be a sinner only when he returns to the passions of worldly existence.

Rabbi Moshe Isserles of Krakow, the Rema, the great posek of the 17th century, supports the Rambam's position. He bases his interpretation, which appears in his book *Toras Haolah*, on the future tense of the words we quoted above, kadosh yihyeh – "he [the נזיר] will become holy." The Rema interprets these words to mean that the נזיר will become holy after he has concluded the period of his vow and returns to normal life. Only then does he live according to the golden rule of the Rambam.

In conclusion, the majority view of the great rabbis and commentators over the centuries is that mortification of the body is not only unnecessary, but sinful. Indeed, there is no legacy of the נזיר after the destruction of Bayis Sheni. נזירים ceased to exist because נזירות can only be fulfilled by sacrificing a korban on the altar of the Beis Hamikdash. The Rambam made it clear that the Torah desires that self-denial be practiced in moderation and not in excess. Ever since, throughout the generations, his golden rule, the middle road, has been followed by the vast majority of religious Jews.

Parashas Beha'aloscha

This week's parashah reveals that רוח הקודש, the Spirit of HaShem, can bring נבואה, prophecy. In Beha'aloscha, we read of three incidents in which prophecy plays a central role. These incidents teach us about the functions of נבואה, demonstrate how HaShem inspires His chosen prophets, and indeed point us to the conclusion that רוח הקודש manifests itself even in our days.

We read that בני ישראל were discontented with their life in the מדבר and expressed with vehemence a desire to return to Egypt. "Moshe heard the people weeping למשפחתיו, in their family groups, each one at the entrance to his tent" (Bamidbar 11:10). Rashi explains that they were frustrated with the restrictions of gilui arayos, forbidden marriage relationships. As a result, ויחר אף ה', "the wrath of HaShem flared greatly," ובעיני משה רע, "and it was bad in the eyes of Moshe" (Bamidbar 11:10).

HaShem, through prophecy, provides a solution to this grave crisis in Moshe's leadership. He tells Moshe, ואצלתי מן הרוח אשר עליך ושמתי עליהם, "Gather together to Me 70 men of the elders of Israel and I will increase some of the Divine Spirit that is upon you and place it upon them" (Bamidbar 11:16-17). This, HaShem did, and the elders prophesied in the camp (Bamidbar 11:25). The Ramban explains how ואצלתי מן הרוח means that the prophetic spirit was taken from Moshe, but Moshe's רוח was not diminished in the least.

Who were these 70 elders? They had been leaders of the Israelite community in Egypt and had protected them when בני ישראל were experiencing cruel bondage. In the מדבר, the people remembered the devotion of the elders, and when they prophesied in the camp, lovingly accepted their proclamations. The nation was spiritually uplifted and once again found belief in HaShem, in Israel and in the Torah.

In the 19th century, Rabbi Samson Raphael Hirsch noted that, in the Tanach, prophecy is generally depicted as a passive act; the verb used is *l'hinabeh*, to be given prophecy. Yet there are instances in which the advent of prophecy is described in a passive-reflexive manner: *l'hisnabeh*, to stimulate oneself to receive prophecy. Such instances occur in this week's parashah where, with regard to the 70 elders, it is written ויתנבאו (Bamidbar 11:25).

A similar instance in which the state of prophetic readiness is described as an emanation of the Holy Spirit from one group or individual to another, can be found in the story of Shaul. We read in Shmuel I 10:10 that a band of prophets came by, at which time Shaul was infused with רוח הקודש. The people who observed his transformation asked a question that became a prophetic adage, הגם שאול בנביאים, "Is Shaul, too, among the prophets?" (Shmuel I 10:11). In this incident, the word for prophecy is also ויתנבא, he caused himself to prophesy.

In this parashah, the second instance of נבואה involves two men, Eldad and Medad, who were not among the 70 chosen elders, about whom it is written, ויתנבאו במחנה, "they prophesied in the camp" (Bamidbar 11:26). Yehoshua bin Nun, the future leader of בני ישראל, came to Moshe and demanded the immediate incarceration of the two. But Moshe responded, "Are you being zealous for my sake? Would that the entire people of HaShem could be prophets, כי יתן ה' רוחו עליהם, if Hashem would but place His Spirit upon them"(Bamidbar 11:29).

We see here that Moshe saw נבואה as a most important way of maintaining Divine Inspiration among בני ישראל. Indeed, he expressed his yearning that all the Children of Israel would attain the status of prophets. The same desire is expressed by Yoel Hanavi, אשפוך את רוחי, "I will pour out My Spirit upon all flesh and your sons and daughters shall prophesy" (Yoel 3:1).

The third incident of נבואה appears at the end of the parashah, when Miriyam and Aharon speak disrespectfully of their brother Moshe. In response, HaShem calls Miriyam and Aharon aside and says, "If there be prophets among you, in a vision shall I, HaShem, make Myself known to him; in a dream shall I speak with him. Not so is my servant Moshe... פה אל פה, mouth to mouth, do I speak to him, in a clear vision and not in riddles" (Bamidbar 12:4-8).Here we learn that whereas all the other prophets are inspired to prophesy through dreams while they are asleep, Moshe's prophecy is unique because HaShem speaks to him when he is fully awake. This is the essential distinction between the prophecy of Moshe Rabbeinu and the messages of all the other prophets. It is perhaps for this reason that the Torah is sometimes called "Toras Moshe."

In thinking about the power of prophecy, we are reminded of the words of the Ramban in his commentary to Shir Hashirim (8:12-13) that the Jews shall return to the Land of Israel. There he writes ואחר כן יבואו הנפוצות המפוזרים בין העמים ושמו להם ראש אחד הוא משיח בן דוד שהיה עמהם בגלות וברשיון מלכי אומות העולם ובעזרתם ילכו לארץ ישראל, "afterwards, those scattered among the nations will come, they will install a leader, namely Mashiach ben David who was with them in exile, and – with the permission of the kings of the nations of the world and with their help – return to ארץ ישראל." Those three predictions almost jump off the page at us today. "The scattered will come" came to pass via the various aliyos in the last two centuries. For the first time since 70 C.E., more Jews live in ארץ ישראל than in the Diaspora. "The permission of the kings of the nations" came to pass via the historic U.N. vote in 1948 recognizing the new Jewish state. The Ramban knew that these would occur and it follows that the Ramban is asserting that Mashiach ben David is with us now. We are in the period of ימות המשיח right now.

נבואה departed from עם ישראל after the destruction of the first Beis Hamikdash (Bava Basra 12a), but just as we read that a spirit of נבואה came to Shaul, prompting the famous question הגם שאול בנביאים, is Shaul too among the prophets, so too we may consider the Ramban's words about the return of עם ישראל to ארץ ישראל to be the expression of רוח הקודש. This is not נבואה but rather it is the power of רוח הקודש which remains in force forever.

It was with similar thoughts that we re-read the words of the Zohar (Vayera), בני ישמעאל עתידים בזמן ההוא לעורר יחד עם כל עמי העולם לבוא לירושלים, "in that time, the sons of Yishmael shall rise up together with all the nations and come to Yerushalayim (for war)." The Zohar predicted that not Bnei Esav but rather Bnei Yishmael will, in the age of אתחלתא דגאולה, go to war against בני ישראל. This has been our very situation since 1948.

נבואה plays an important part in this parashah and in all of Jewish history. Although HaShem took prophecy away from עם ישראל after the destruction of the Beis Hamikdash, He bestows רוח הקודש throughout the ages.

Parashas Shelach

The central theme in Parashas Shelach is the lack of faith in HaShem expressed by the Jewish people and their leaders as they prepared to conquer ארץ ישראל. Instead of relying on השגחה, providence, as promised by HaShem, they willingly accepted the falsified and misleading report of the 10 men that Moshe had sent to spy out the Land.

The Torah tells us that these spies were distinguished men, princes of their fathers' tribes, each one a leader (Bamidbar 13:2). Rashi comments that they were all members of the Sanhedrin, the greatest talmidei chachamim of their generation (Rashi on Bamidbar 14:1). They were gedolei yisrael, the Torah leadership of the nation.

The sin of the spies was that they lacked אמונה, faith in HaShem. בני ישראל accepted that which the spies reported: "We are not able to go up against the people [in the Land] for they are stronger ממנו – than we" (Bamidbar 13:31). The word ממנו in Hebrew can refer either to the first person plural "we," or the third person singular "he." Rashi quotes the Gemara in asserting that the spies meant to say that "they," i.e., the people of the land of Canaan, were stronger than "He," i.e., HaShem.

The incident of the spies is the earliest example of the inner weakness in relation to the Land of Israel often shown by the Jewish people and their leaders. Throughout history, Jews have often felt a certain reluctance when the subject of actually returning to ארץ ישראל was raised.

A reluctance to return to ארץ ישראל manifested itself following the destruction of the first Beis Hamikdash. After 70 years in Babylon, very few exiles returned to ארץ ישראל. The Book of Ezra records that only 42,360 men came back from the Babylonian exile (Ezra 2:64). In *The Kuzari*, Yehuda Halevi (11th century) writes that the rich and the learned did not return from Babylon to Israel (Kuzari 2:24).

Despite this ambivalence, ארץ ישראל and Yerushalayim remained engraved in the memories and in the hearts of the nation. This allegiance expressed itself in the daily prayers and in fervent hopes for גאולה שלימה final redemption. But Yehuda Halevi, who expressed his love for the homeland in his immortal love poems for Zion, was an exception in that he did return to ארץ ישראל. In fact he died, upon arrival, על קידוש ה'.

The *Zohar*, which appeared in the 14th century, sharply criticizes the 10 spies, who, although they were גדולי ישראל, nevertheless spoke against the Land. In the מדבר they served as leaders of their generation, but they were fearful that, with the conquest of the Holy Land, their own כבוד, the honor and respect they enjoyed, would decline; these are the selfish considerations ascribed to them by the *Zohar*. (Parashas Shelach, Mosad Rav Kook: Book 3, 158:1) In the 18th century, the tzaddik and mystic R. Chaim Attar (1686-1743), in his commentary *Ohr HaChayim* (Vayikra 25:25), expressed similarly critical opinions of גדולי ישראל in his own age.

In the early 20th century, the Jewish relationship to ארץ ישראל was still undecided. For fully 400 years, the Jews of Eastern Europe had suffered constant pogroms and persecution, and in many regions they were increasingly impoverished. At that time, before the British Mandate, it was relatively easy to immigrate to ארץ ישראל. A mostly secular group comprised the first aliyot. Later, as anti-Semitism and Nazism strengthened, religious Jews also joined the aliyot.

History has shown that those who opposed the Zionist idea worked under incorrect assumptions. The State of Israel has brought new life to the Jewish people. Israel's successes over the past 65 years are phenomenal. The fact of kibbutz galuyos, the ingathering of the Diaspora of six million Jews, and the outstanding growth and development of Torah study throughout ארץ ישראל are a sign that HaShem has blessed all those who are living their lives to build and defend the Holy Land, a vindication min hashamayim that we are living in the age of ראשית צמיחת גאולתנו – the beginning of the flowering of our Redemption – as described in the Prayer for the State of Israel in the Torah service every Shabbos.

In conclusion, let us pay tribute to the Gadol haDor of the last century, R' Yisrael Meir Kagan, the Chafetz Chayim (1838-1933). In 1933, just before he passed away and shortly after the Nazis had come to power in Germany, worried students asked him, "What future has the Jewish people?" He responded by quoting the book of Yoel, בהר ציון ובירושלים תהיה פליטה, "on the Mount of Zion and in Yerushalayim there shall be refuge" (Yoel. 3:5). Renewal would come in the Land of Israel; the future of the Jewish people is in Yerushalayim. Like Yehoshua bin Nun and Kalev ben Yefuneh, he was unshakeable in his belief that the destiny of the Jewish people is in ארץ ישראל.

In fact, many of the great tzaddikim of the Hasidic world had a positive opinion regarding Israel; among them the Gerer Rebbe, the Sokochover Rebbe and the Boyaner Rebbe. (These and many more are listed in *HaTekufah HaGedolah*). The late Lubavitcher Rebbe declared that Israel's victory in 1967 was a nes min hashamayim. We learn from this parashah the central importance of the Land of Israel and today's State of Israel to Jewish people everywhere.

Parashas Korach

This parashah tells the story of Korach, who instigated a rebellion against the Divine authority of his cousin, Moshe Rabbeinu. For their insolence, Korach and his cohorts suffered a unique punishment: The earth opened up and swallowed them all (Bamidbar 16:32).

Before his rebellion, Korach was one of the most prominent men of his day (Midrash Rabbah 18:8). He was a Levite and of the family of Kehas, whose task it was to carry the Aron Hakodesh during Israel's wanderings in the מדבר. The *Midrash* says that he possessed רוח הקודש, the Divine Spirit, and his children composed outstanding psalms. They wrote nine psalms, including Psalm 47, which we recite on Rosh Hashannah before תקיעת שופר, and which starts, למנצח לבני קרח מזמור, "for the conductor, by the sons of Korach, a Psalm."

However, Korach was possessed of uncontrollable ambition, unquenchable envy and insatiable jealousy, and these inspired in him an insolent thirst for power that, in the end, caused his spectacular downfall. His fate is an illustration of the Jewish belief that great men often have an equally great יצר הרע, evil inclination (*Tikkun Zohar* 13).

Korach exclaimed, רב לכם, "It is too much for you" – Moshe and Aharon, you have taken too much authority for yourselves! He then spoke words that struck at the very heart of Moshe's legitimacy as leader: "For the entire assembly, כלם קדשים, all of them are holy, and HaShem is among them; why do you exalt yourselves over the congregation of HaShem?" (Bamidbar 16:3).

At first glance, it appears that Korach raised a reasonable question. HaShem chose all of the Jewish people, and all are thus equally holy. But a deeper understanding reveals that Korach completely and deviously misrepresented the concept of kedushah, sanctity, for there are two different ways in which kedushah finds expression.

The first type of kedushah, קדושת ישראל, is an innate characteristic of בני ישראל. HaShem's act of creating the Jewish people is identical to His act of choosing the Jewish people – that is, bestowing upon them kedushah. HaShem created us kedoshim, holy individuals, imbuing us with a holiness that is innate to the entire assembly of Israel.

However, in contrast to Korach's impudent assertion, this type of kedushah is bestowed in unequal measure: most of it is conferred on the Kohanim, a lesser amount on the Leviim, and the rest on Yisrael.

The second, complimentary, type of kedushah can be earned by every Jew who, by his own will and effort, lifts himself up spiritually by striving to reach out to HaShem. חז״ל promise that HaShem comes near to all who seek Him. According to the Gemara, HaShem declared, אם תבא אל ביתי אני אבא אל ביתך, אם לא תבא אל ביתי אני לא אבא אל ביתך, "if you come to my house, I will come to your house. If you do not come to my house, I will not come to your house" (Sukkah 53a).

This type of kedushah, which can be more powerful than the sanctity that HaShem has made inherent in בני ישראל, is also conferred in unequal measure. However, its unequal distribution is solely the result of an individual's striving, or lack thereof, to bring himself closer to HaShem. The greater the effort, the greater the kedushah that is bestowed. In other words, each person is enriched with holiness in direct proportion to the exertion he expends to attain it.

By way of illustration, the Mishnah (Horayos 3:8) tells us, ממזר תלמיד חכם קודם לכהן גדול עם הארץ, that if a ממזר, someone who has no personal status at all in Judaism, becomes learned in Torah through his own effort, then he shall have preference even over the high priest, if the high priest is ignorant in Torah knowledge.

Not only the Jewish people but all of mankind have the opportunity to draw near to HaShem through action and effort. *Tanna D'bei Eliyahu* writes, "I call heaven and earth to witness that whether it be a heathen or a Jew, whether it be a man or a woman, manservant or maidservant, the Holy Spirit will suffuse each of them in keeping with the deeds he or she performs" (Midrash Eliyahu Raba, chapter 9 (10), page 152).

Similarly, the Rambam, at the end of Hilchos Shmitah VeYovel (13:13), writes that a person from any of the nations of the world who dedicates his will and spirit to stand before HaShem is to be considered קודש קדושים, the holy of the holiest.

These sources provide a tremendous insight into the nature of holiness. The distribution of kedushah may be unequal, but it can be attained by every human being. It is universal in its application.

In conclusion, what was the sin of Korach? In confronting Moshe, he made the incendiary assertion כלם קדשים, that all of Israel are no more and no less holy than Moshe and Aharon. In so doing, he willfully and self-servingly ignored the unequal distribution of innate kedushah between the Kohanim, Leviim and Yisraelim. In addition, he ignored the difference between individuals – of all nations – who have striven to come close to HaShem and on whom HaShem, based on their merit, has bestowed kedushah equal to their effort.

In his rebellion against Moshe, Korach contradicted HaShem who had already said, לא כן עבדי משה, "not so is My servant Moshe, in My entire house he is the trusted one." (Bamidbar 12:7). Moshe was unique; no person was, is, or ever will be equal to him. This was the unforgivable sin committed by Korach.

Parashas Chukas

The predominant theme of the Book of Bamidbar is the trials and tribulations encountered by בני ישראל in the wilderness on their way from Egypt to the Holy Land. Somewhat surprisingly, however, Parashas Chukas opens with a detailed description of the laws of the פרה אדומה, the red heifer, which functioned to purify a person who had become טמא – halachically unclean – by touching a corpse. Such an individual could return to a state of ritual purity by being sprinkled with water mixed with the ashes of the red heifer. What is the connection between this act of purification and the wanderings of Israel in the מדבר?

Conquering ארץ ישראל was the ultimate test of the readiness of בני ישראל to become a nation. In Egypt, they lived for generations as slaves, without hope, without ideals and without responsibilities. In the מדבר, they acted like the simple slaves they had so recently been, yearning for their former lives in Egypt, which required only that they obey their taskmasters. בני ישראל refused to take on responsibility for themselves, either as individuals or as a nation, a prerequisite for achieving a higher spiritual level and for serving HaShem as an עם סגולה – a unique nation – and, on a more practical level, for conquering ארץ ישראל.

The purification of people who are טמא because of contact with a corpse was a necessary part of the preparation of בני ישראל for their entry into the Holy Land. They knew that they faced war against the seven nations that lived in the Land and had to prepare for the realities that they would encounter in a military campaign. This parashah records the war against the Canaanites (Bamidbar 21:1-3), as well as the battles with Sihon, King of the Emorites (Bamidbar 21:23-24) and Og, King of Bashan (Bamidbar 21:35).

In the context of the parashah, Abarbanel cites the Gemara, ה׳ מקדים רפואה למכה, "HaShem sends the remedy before the plague" (Megillah 13b). Before the beginning of the conquest of ארץ ישראל, HaShem gave Israel the means to purify itself from the contamination caused by contact with the dead. It is worth noting that the act of purification described in this parashah also initiates a process of healing the inner turmoil of the soldier who may face danger, possible death and killing others during battle.

Shlomo Hamelech, the wisest person ever born, declares in Koheles, "All this I tested with wisdom; I thought I could become wise, but it is beyond me" (Koheles 7:23). King Solomon acquired all human wisdom, including the wisdom of the Torah. Nevertheless, according to חז"ל, the secret of the פרה אדומה eluded him. Seforno (16th century, Italy) sums up the contradiction inherent in the process of purification, מטהר את הטמאים ומטמא את הטהורים, the process causes purification of the impure while simultaneously rendering impure that which is pure. When the ashes of the red heifer, mixed with water, are sprinkled on a person who is טמא, he becomes purified, but the individual who sprinkles the ashes becomes impure, albeit to a lesser degree. Thus the mystery: how does that which transforms impurity into purity also perform the precisely opposite process at the same time? Was there impurity in the purifying water? This is what Shlomo, the wise king, could not understand.

Life and death are mysteries that belong only to HaShem. So, too, is the spiritual matter of purifying a person who is טמא. Thus, the mitzvah of the פרה אדומה is a chok – a Divine commandment that the holy nation accepts without being provided an explanation. This process is beyond the realm of human understanding.

We may gain some insights into this phenomenon by looking at another incident involving Divinely ordained conquest. The Torah tells us that King David paid a high price as a result of having carried out his assigned task of vanquishing the enemies of Israel in order to conquer ארץ ישראל. When he aspired to build the Beis HaMikdash, HaShem told him that he could not do so because שפכת דם לרב, "You spilled much blood" (Divre

Yamim I 22:8). That sacred task would be left to his son and successor, King Solomon. At first glance, HaShem's statement seems puzzling: Is it a sin to spill the blood of an enemy in battle? Should David not have fought the foes of Israel?

Certainly, David did not commit a sin by killing the enemies of Israel. All the wars he fought were מלחמות ה׳, wars of HaShem. We find confirmation of this from Avigail, a prophetess, who told King David, "for my lord fights all the wars of HaShem, and no blame has been found in you in your days" (Shmuel 1 25:28). Yet, despite this, David did not merit to fulfill the mitzvah of building the Beis HaMikdash. This is because killing, even when Divinely ordained, harms the soul.

We are a nation that is bound up with HaShem by the mitzvos. Consequently, we must distance ourselves from sin and טומאה. HaShem is the Ribono shel Olam, the Absolute Master of the Universe and all that is within it. He creates the good as well as the bad. As we read in Yeshayahu, עשה שלום ובורא רע, "He makes peace and creates evil" (Yeshayahu 45:7). Some mitzvos require acts from which we must later be purified. King David was exposed to great violence in conquering the Land, as ordained by HaShem, but he could not be purified and was therefore not permitted to construct the center of kedushah in this world. However, בני ישראל, who would inevitably be exposed to the טומאה of death in their Divinely ordained conquest of ארץ ישראל, are presented in this week's parashah with the promise of purification.

Parashas Balak

The strange figure of Bilam, presented in Parashas Balak, and his four Divinely inspired berachos, blessings, of בני ישראל require a great deal of explanation. Bilam first appears as an evil sorcerer who intends to bring destruction upon Israel, either by sorcery or the evil eye. Slowly, his malicious inclinations weaken until they totally disappear, and he is inspired by HaShem to serve – at this particular moment in time – in the capacity of a true prophet.

Bilam blessed בני ישראל in four blessings, inspired by HaShem.

The first blessing contains the phrase הן עם לבדד ישכן ובגוים לא יתחשב, "behold, it is a nation that will dwell in solitude, and not be reckoned amongst the nations" (Bamidbar 23:9). Rashi, referring to this verse and to the segulah, uniqueness, of Israel, writes, "Israel is the only nation which will not cease to exist." Ibn Ezra says, "Just like this nation is isolated and alone now in the מדבר, so will Israel remain separate and alone with the Torah and their laws." Because of HaShem's unique providence, no other nation will have the power to permanently overwhelm Israel. The Ramban and Abarbanel stress the unique difference that separates Israel from other nations: Israel is the only national entity in the world whose religion and nationhood are indivisible.

In 1961, Dr. Yaakov Herzog, son of the former Chief Rabbi of Israel, Rav Yitchak Herzog, challenged the eminent English historian Arnold Toynbee to a public debate in Montreal. Toynbee had declared that the Jews are a fossil remnant and therefore have no place among the nations of the modern world. Toynbee claimed that the Jewish people ceased to exist as a nation 2,000 years ago. Dr. Herzog, in his rhetorical victory over Toynbee, quoted a verse from Parashas Balak, עם לבדד ישכן. Israel shall dwell separately, alone among the nations, but will live on for eternity.

The second prophetic blessing of Bilam is that the wanderings in the מדבר of בני ישראל will come to an end. בני ישראל will then enter the Land and dwell in it. This berachah begins with the words, "HaShem is not man to be capricious, or mortal to change His mind..." – ההוא אמר ולא יעשה ודבר ולא יקימנה, "Would He speak and not act, promise and not fulfill?" (Bamidbar 23:19). Seforno sees in this pasuk a hint of how Israel should conduct themselves during the period of the conquest, expelling the inhabitants of ארץ ישראל but not destroying them. As the Yerushalmi states and the Rambam confirms, Yehoshua offered three choices to שבעת העמים, the seven nations dwelling in Canaan: Whoever wished to leave could do so; those who wanted to stay could do so on condition that they accepted the seven Noahide Laws; and those who wished to go to war could choose confrontation. But if the enemies of Israel chose war, concluded Bilam, they would be defeated: "Behold! The people will arise like a lion cub and raise itself like a lion. It will not lie down until it consumes prey, and drinks the blood of the slain" (Bamidbar 23:24). The Ramban interprets this verse to refer to the conquest of the land during the period of Yehoshua, when בני ישראל would defeat and kill powerful kings.

The third prophetic blessing of Bilam is מה טבו אהליך יעקב, "How goodly are your tents, O Yaakov, your dwelling places, O Israel" (Bamidbar 24:5). Commentators over the generations have offered various explanations of this verse. Rabbi Bachiya (13th century, Spain) presented a simple interpretation: That Bilam is describing the future dwellings of בני ישראל after their return to the Land of Israel. To Abarbanel, this blessing looks forward to a time when בני ישראל will not only settle ארץ ישראל and populate it but will build the Beis Hamikdash and destroy the seed of Amalek. Many other Rishonim write in a similar vein.

The third blessing specifically mentions Agag, the king of Amalek, who was slain by the prophet Shmuel, so it would appear that Bilam's vision refers to the Kingdom of David, established after the death of Agag.

The fourth and final prophecy of Bilam is that in the End of Days HaShem will grace Israel by bringing redemption through the Mashiach. The word of HaShem is expressed through Bilam, "I shall see him but not now, I shall look at him, but it is not near. A star has issued from Yaakov and a scepter-bearer has risen from Israel" (Bamidbar 24:17). The Rambam states at the end of Hilchos Melachim (11:1) that this pasuk is the Torah source for the coming of the Mashiach. It refers both to the kingdom of David and to the future Mashiach in the End of Days. Based on this pasuk, the Rambam wrote in his famous Thirteen Articles of Faith, אני מאמין באמונה שלמה בביאת המשיח, "I believe with perfect faith in the coming of the Mashiach." This is so central as to be included in the Siddur at the end of Shacharis.

In summary, we find that each of Bilam's four prophecies expressed HaShem's destiny for Israel. The first promised that, thanks to HaShem's providence, בני ישראל will continue to exist until the End of Days. The second foresaw that Israel would succeed in conquering ארץ ישראל. The third anticipated the establishment of the Kingdom of David and the fourth foresaw the establishment of the Kingdom of Mashiach.

Parashas Pinchas

At the end of Parashas Balak, an outraged Pinchas takes a spear and carries out summary justice in response to an act of brazen immorality. The first psukim of Parashas Pinchas demonstrate HaShem's endorsement of Pinchas' actions and his קנאות, zealotry. "HaShem spoke to Moshe, saying: 'Pinchas... turned back My wrath from upon the Children of Israel when he zealously avenged Me...' Therefore say, הנני נתן לו את בריתי שלום, 'Behold! I give him My covenant of peace'" (Bamidbar 25:10-12).

However, according to חז"ל, the response of the Children of Israel to Pinchas was many-sided. In the Gemara, we read that the 12 tribes shamed Pinchas by pointing out that his maternal grandfather, Yisro, had been a Midianite priest who fattened sheep before they were sacrificed to idols – and yet he had dared to kill a prince of Israel, Zimri ben Salu (Sanhedrin 82b). And the Yerushalmi (Sanhedrin 9:7) says that Pinchas acted in opposition to the will of חז"ל, who would have put him under cherem had a heavenly voice not declared that Pinchas and his seed shall have ברית כהנת עולם, "a covenant of eternal priesthood" (Bamidbar 25:13).

According to the Gemara, the people suspected that Pinchas' zealotry was tinged with aggression, a trait that is characteristic of idol worshippers, who are not only mistaken in their concept of the Divine but are profoundly corrupt, sexually immoral and given to violence, which they even bring into their sanctuaries. Pinchas, as we know, was a descendent of Yisro, a priest to the idol worshippers of Midian, before he joined the Jewish people. Yet, despite Yisro's conversion, the people suspected that a violent streak had remained in the soul and character of Pinchas. It is for this reason that the Torah proclaims the purity of Pinchas' descent. The formula "Pinchas, son of Elazar, son of Aharon the Cohen" emphasizes that Pinchas is of the seed of Aharon, an אוהב שלום ורודף שלום, "a lover of peace and pursuer of peace," and an איש שלום, a true man of peace whose soul knows nothing of violence.

In the same place in Sanhedrin, we also find a discussion of the legality of Pinchas' act. "Said Rav, 'Pinchas saw what was being done and reminded himself of the law thereof and then asked Moshe Rabbeinu. Moshe answered him, "let he who dictates the letter be its carrier."'" That is, Moshe sanctioned the slaying of Zimri ben Salu. According to this opinion, Pinchas' act required – and received – the personal approval of Moshe, emphasizing that it was not done impulsively or with impure motives. The portrayal of this incident in the Talmud demonstrates that קנאות, zealotry, and the intentions and motives of its proponents, must be considered critically.

This week's haftarah, which concerns Eliyahu the prophet, also conveys the lesson that all acts of קנאות, even those performed by the most holy of men, are suspect. Eliyahu and Pinchas, among our tradition's most famous קנאים, zealots, have similar souls, so much so that the Midrash Rabbah on Shir Hashirim states, Pinchas ze Eliyahu, "Pinchas is Eliyahu". Pinchas and Eliyahu share the same destinies.

While Eliyahu was fleeing Izevel, who was trying to kill him, "the word of HaShem came to him and said to him, 'why are you here, Eliyahu?' He answered, קנא קנאתי לה', 'I have acted with great zeal for HaShem, HaShem of Legions, for the Children of Israel have forsaken Your covenant; they have razed Your altars and have killed Your prophets by the sword, so that I alone have remained, and they now seek to take my life' " (Melachim 1 19:9-10). We see that Eliyahu's קנאות for HaShem is mixed with the rage and survival instinct of a man pursued. His intentions are not pure.

Three hours later, according to חז"ל, HaShem again asks Eliyahu the same question: "'Why are you here, Elihayu?'" And Eliyhau answers exactly as before (Melachim 1 19:13-14), still pleading for his personal safety. That is, he is still motivated by factors other than his loyalty to HaShem. HaShem's response to Eliyahu's impure zealotry is drastic: He recalls him from prophetic service and instructs him, ואת אלישע בן שפט... תמשח

לנביא תחתיך, "Anoint Elisha, the son of Shafat... as a prophet in your stead'" (Melachim I 19:16). HaShem herewith instructs Eliyahu that he is to give up his service as prophet.

Eliyahu is portrayed in Haftaras Pinchas as a great zealot (see Parashas Tzav / Shabbos Hagadol), yet in Acharis HaYamim, at the End of Days, he shall reappear as the Angel of Peace. In the haftarah of Shabbos Hagadol, we read in the book of Malachi, the last of the prophets, הנה אנכי שלח לכם את אליה הנביא, "Behold, I send you the prophet Eliyahu before the coming of the great and awesome day of HaShem. And he will turn back [to HaShem] the hearts of the fathers with [their] sons, and the hearts of the sons with their fathers" (Malachi 3:23-24).

In conclusion, in Haftaras Pinchas Eliyahu undergoes a transformation. After speaking and behaving in a manner befitting only a קנאי HaShem intervenes, relieving Eliyahu of his duties as a prophet and bringing him up to Heaven in a fiery chariot (Melachim II 2:11). When Eliyahu next appears, in the book of Malachi, he is a man of peace, turning fathers and sons to each other and to HaShem. Whereas Eliyahu's zealotry as a prophet was tinged with personal interest, at the End of Days he will be an emissary of love and peace for Israel and the world. Similarly, at the very end of last week's parashah, Pinchas demonstrated the intolerant and fiery temperament of a zealot and yet, at the beginning of this week's parashah, HaShem declares, "Behold I give him My covenant of peace" (Bamidbar 25:12).

Parashas Mattos-Masei

Parashas Masei concludes the book of Bamidbar by bringing עם ישראל to the end of its wanderings in the מדבר. It also highlights, as the people stand on the banks of the Jordan River, that they are about to cross into ארץ ישראל and therefore must receive the mitzvos concerning the Holy Land. In that way, Parashas Masei is not about wandering, but rather dwelling, that is to say living in the Land.

In this parashah, we find the מצוות עשה, the positive commandments, both to conquer ארץ ישראל and to dwell in it, והורשתם את הארץ וישבתם בה כי לכם נתתי את הארץ לרשת אתה, and you shall possess the Land and settle in it, for to you have I given the Land to possess it" (Bamidbar 33:53). The parashah also specifies the gevulos, borders, of ארץ ישראל, emphasizing that "this is the Land that shall fall to you as an inheritance" (Bamidbar 34:2) As with any inheritance, this one has specific dimensions and is an inheritance that belongs to עם ישראל for eternity and cannot ever be handed over or sold to non-Jews. This is clearly stated by the Rambam (Hilchos Avodah Zarah 10:3).

The Ramban says that עם ישראל was commanded not only to conquer the Land, but also to defend it; that is, never to leave it in the hands of other nations or to abandon it as a wilderness (*Sefer Hamitzvos Leminyan Haramban*, Mitzvos Aseh, Mitzvah Four). From these words – indeed, from the Torah itself – it is clear that עם ישראל is commanded to set up a state with an organized government and to form an army. It is a mitzvah incumbent on the men of all the tribes – except Shevet Levi – to serve as soldiers, both to conquer ארץ ישראל and, then, to defend it.

After בני ישראל came into the Land, and after the establishment of מלכות דוד, the Kingdom of David, the era of the first Beis Hamikdash came to an abrupt end in 586 B.C.E. with Galus Bavel, the Babylonian Exile. According to the Gemara (Yoma 9b), the חורבן, destruction, of the Beis Hamikdash was caused by the three cardinal transgressions committed by בני ישראל: עבודה זרה, idol worship; שפיכות דמים, bloodshed; and גילוי עריות, forbidden sexual relationships. Two generations later, the Persian ruler, Cyrus, allowed בני ישראל to return to ארץ ישראל. Unfortunately, only 42,360 Jews (Ezra 2:64) made aliyah; the rich and the learned remained in Babylon. As we all know, the second Beis Hamikdash was destroyed by the Romans in the year 70 C.E. The Gemara says that the reason for this חורבן was שנאת חינם, hatred without cause. This sin was not quickly forgiven, and עם ישראל had to wait almost until our day – nearly 2,000 years – to return en masse to the Land of Israel.

In the early 1800s, nearly a century before the Zionist movement, communities of religious Jews from Eastern Europe – both followers of the Vilna Gaon and the hasidim of the Baal Shem Tov – made aliyah to ארץ ישראל, settling in Yerushalayim and Tzfat. They did not cultivate the land. In fact, these two groups were known as the perushim, "separates" because their focus was concentrated exclusively on spiritual progress and Torah study.

However, in the late 1800s, the Zionist movement commenced the great return of the Jewish people to the Land of Israel. The vast majority of these first olim were secular and made aliyah in order to drain the swamps and establish agricultural settlements, in many cases risking their own lives. After World War I, it became relatively easy for Jews to make aliyah because the British had yet to limit immigration or land sales and the Arabs had not yet declared their opposition to Zionism. Tragically, few religious Jews took advantage of this opportunity. In 1931, German Jews established the first religious kibbutz known as Rodges, which was ultimately named Yavneh. In 1933, the Nazis rose to power, which precipitated an aliyah that included religious Jews.

After World War II and the Shoah, the new State of Israel, under the leadership of David Ben Gurion, displayed ahavas chinam – exemplary love without reason or recompense – as it accepted every Jew who needed refuge, including survivors of the camps, the sick, the poor, the old, the broken – with love and devotion. Under Chok HaShvut, the Law of Return, Israel has continued to welcome any Jew regardless of background, color or financial situation.

Among those who played a leading role in building the pre-state yishuv and the State of Israel were the followers of Rav Avraham Yizhak HaKohen Kook (1865-1935), who would become the first Chief Ashkenazi Rabbi of the State of Israel. He was deeply inspired by the work of the חלוצים , pioneers, whom he regarded as instruments of HaShem's plan for geulah, redemption, despite their irreligious behavior. As a mystic, he saw external events as symbols of a deeper, hidden reality; to him, the actions of the חלוצים were part of the cosmic process of restoring harmony to a fragmented world. As a result, he understood the secular Zionists to be part of a greater providential design in returning עם ישראל to ארץ ישראל.

This parashah is a reminder for us to look at the words of ברכת החדש, the Blessing of the New Month, in which we say: הוא יגאל, אותנו בקרוב ויקבץ נדחנו מארבע כנפות הארץ חברים כל ישראל, "HaShem will redeem us soon and gather in our dispersed from the four corners of the Earth; all Israel becoming חברים." What is a חבר? Someone well-versed in Torah and its practice. Today, over six million Jews have returned to Israel from the four corners of the Earth and, b'ezras HaShem, more will come. This week's parashah describes עם ישראל as it stood on the verge of entering the Land. In our day, we are fortunate to witness a thriving Jewish state that not only supports great universities and world-class technologies but is also blessed with a flourishing religious life and the greatest concentration of Torah study that the Jewish people has ever known.

5 SEFER DEVARIM

Parashas Devarim

The haftarah for Parashas Devarim is the first chapter of Yeshayahu. This parashah always precedes Tisha b'Av and is therefore called Shabbos Chazon, the Shabbos of the Great Rebuke. The first verse of the haftarah mentions four kings who lived contemporaneously with Yeshayahu Hanavi, the last of whom was Chizkiyahu HaMelech. He was the most pious king; he led a veritable revolution of the population to return to HaShem, to fulfill mitzvos and to study the Torah.

The major aspect of this prophecy in Yeshayahu, however, is about a society that had rebelled against HaShem. The haftarah describes them as מכף רגל ועד ראש אין בו מתם, "from the sole of the foot to the head, nothing in them is whole" (Yeshayahu.1:6). Yet the Gemara says about that era that "no boy or girl, man or woman was found who was not fully versed in the laws of tumah and taharah" (Sanhedrin 94b). How can we resolve the description of a rebellious people in Sefer Yeshayahu with the description of a pious people in Sanhedrin? It is very strange to find the description of such a corrupt society in the days of Chizkiyahu who, as mentioned above, is regarded as a great king who brought Israel back to Torah life.

To understand this, we have to remember the difference between מצוות בין אדם למקום, mitzvos between man and HaShem, and מצוות בין אדם לחברו, mitzvos between man and man, as discussed in Parashas Mishpatim. The words of Yeshayahu HaNavi make this clear. He rebukes Israel by saying: "Why do I need your numerous sacrifices? When you come to appear before me, who sought this from your hand, to trample my courtyards. חדשיכם ומועדיכם שנאה נפשי, My soul detests your new moons and your appointed times; they become a burden upon me. When you spread your hands before me in prayer, I will hide my eyes from you, I will not listen, your hands are replete with blood. Wash yourselves, purify yourselves. Learn to do good, seek justice, vindicate the victim, render justice to the orphan, take up the grievance of the widow" (1:11-17).

These psukim declare the importance of observing the mitzvos that are בין אדם לחברו. Yeshayahu Hanavi clearly explains that people may consider themselves religious from a technical standpoint, but HaShem is not to be found amongst them. It is reasonable, then, to conclude that Israel under Chizkiyahu HaMelech would have meticulously observed the mitzvos בין אדם למקום, for example tumah and taharah, but fallen short of observing interpersonal mitzvos.

By using the strong language of "hating" your מועדים, the navi here tries to explain the distaste of HaShem for worship that comes from hands which are stained with corruption and immoral behavior. The haftarah teaches us that mitzvos בין אדם לחברו are paramount. A community in which HaShem dwells concentrates its energies on both spiritual improvement and justice; neither can be at the expense of the other.

We mourn on Tisha b'Av not only the destruction of the first Beis Hamikdash in 586 B.C.E., but also the destruction of the second Beis Hamikdash in the year 70 C.E. There is a proof that graphically illustrates that ignoring mitzvos between man and man and the absence of love for one's fellow man leads to sinas chinam, baseless hatred. In the famous story of Kamza and Bar Kamza (Gittin 55b), Bar Kamza brings false evidence to the Roman emperor that the Jews are rebelling against him. He does it as revenge for having been offended by a man who mistakenly invited him to a party, thinking he was the similarly named Kamza, and then publicly humiliated him.

We should note that the first Beis Hamikdash was destroyed as a result of the sin of idol worship, which is a sin between man and HaShem. The second Beis Hamikdash was destroyed as a result of the sin of baseless hatred, a violation between man and man.

Baruch HaShem, we have returned to our national homeland in ארץ ישראל with the legal approval of the nations of the world. This is an indication that the sins that caused Israel's exile have been forgiven and that the flaws in the character of the Jewish people are being repaired. Israel is now found capable to govern its people in righteousness, integrity and honesty of purpose. The Israeli legal system will prosecute any individual, including members of the government, who is accused of corruption – even the president. Widows and orphans are protected in the courts of Israel. This reality signals the beginning of the Flowering of the Redemption. Let us work on our own middos and hope and pray that we shall be worthy to witness the building of the third Beis Hamikdash and the Geulah Shaleimah.

Parashas Va'eschanan

Last week was Shabbos Chazon, the Shabbos of Rebuke. We read how Yeshayahu HaNavi chastised the Jewish people for their sins and alienation from HaShem. Yeshayahu's prophecy on this Shabbos, שבת נחמו, is just the opposite. The haftarah read with Parashas Va'eschanan is the first of a series of seven haftaros that are read in the seven weeks after Tisha b'Av leading up to Rosh Hashanah. These haftaros seek to comfort Israel following their return to Yerushalayim from the 70 years of exile in Babylon. Therefore they are called the שבעה דנחמתא, the seven haftaros of consolation.

In the haftarah of שבת נחמו, the great prophet offers a vision of consolation and deliverance embodied in a return to the Land and renewed closeness to HaShem. The nevuah begins with the words, נחמו נחמו עמי, "Comfort ye, comfort ye, My People, says HaShem. Speak to the heart of Yerushalayim and proclaim to her that her time for exile has been fulfilled. That her iniquity has been conciliated, for she has received from the hand of HaShem double punishment for all her sins"(Yeshayahu. 40:1-2).

Here the navi states that the Jewish people deserve a double portion of comfort because they have endured a double portion of suffering, not only the destruction of the Beis Hamikdash in Yerushalayim, but also exile to a foreign land. The double portion of comfort refers to the end of the exile and the rebuilding of the Beis Hamikdash in Yerushalayim. Later in the haftarah we read that the navi proclaims this Divine message: על הר גבוה עלי לך, "Get to a high mountain, pronounce to Zion... Say to the cities of Yehudah 'Behold your G-d!' HaShem comes with great power... Behold his reward is with Him... Like a shepherd feeds his flock... [He] gathers the lambs in his arms..." (Yeshayahu 40:9-11).

Yeshayahu explains that HaShem is with all Jews at all times. Likening HaShem to a good shepherd, the prophet describes how the Holy One Blessed be He will lead Israel out of exile slowly and gently, supporting every sick and suffering person until they reach Zion and rebuild the holy Beis Hamikdash. In this way, HaShem will doubly comfort the Jewish people after they have suffered a double portion of punishment for their sins.

In his book *Nesivos Shalom*, Rabbi Shalom Noach Berezovsky of Slonim (1911-2000) cites the founding rebbe of the Slonimer dynasty, who offers an interesting explanation to the question of the source of the consolation. He reads the verse as follows, " 'Comfort ye, comfort ye' – says who? Says your G-d." The comfort lies in the fact that G-d Almighty says that Israel is His nation. Despite all of its sins and alienations, HaShem declares that Israel remains His chosen nation. All Jews are part of this nation. No Jew is excluded, nor is any Jew ever forsaken by HaShem, even in the darkest of times. HaShem is with all Jews at all times. This is the greatest of all consolations.

This idea is reflected in another passage. In Devarim 14:1, we read בנים אתם לה אלקיכם, "You are children to HaShem, your G-d." This pasuk is further expounded upon in the Talmud (Kiddushin 36a), which records a debate between two sages regarding the implication of the pasuk. According to Rabbi Yehudah, when Israel behaves מנהג בנים, as loyal children following the Torah, they are designated as HaShem's children. However, Rabbi Meir says that whether or not Israel behaves, מנהג בנים, following the Torah or not following the Torah, they are still all called the children of HaShem. The founding rebbe of the Slonimer dynasty stated that the halachah follows Rabbi Meir so that in fact, whether Israel's behavior is exemplary or not, they are still designated as His children.

This, then, is the explanation of the repetition of the words נחמו נחמו עמי, be comforted that you are part of Ami – My nation. In other words, whatever the circumstances, I am your G-d, and be comforted that you are the children of HaShem. The status of children remains unchanged forever. The relationship of parents to children is of a permanent nature and is not subject to change. Even if the children become sinful and alienated, they remain children of their father.

This ineradicable bond between HaShem and Israel is further reflected in the parashah itself, in which we find the repetition of the Ten Commandments. In Parashas Mishpatim (Shemos 24:12), Rashi quotes Midrash Rabbah (Bamidbar Rabbah 13:16), which states that all of the 613 mitzvos are contained in the Ten Commandments. Furthermore, with regard to the relationship between the Torah, HaShem and His children, The *Zohar* states, קודשא בריך הוא, ישראל, ואורייתא חד הוא, "Israel, Torah and the Holy One Blessed Be He are one" (Parashas Vayikra 73, see Parashas Bamidbar). This means that HaShem, the Torah and Israel are together an inseparable and indivisible unit. The Torah binds Israel and HaShem together.

In conclusion, while the haftarah of Nachamu speaks about HaShem and Israel, it is the parashah that provides the link of the inseparable unit of HaShem-Torah-Israel. To the Jew who behaves as HaShem's child, the Torah is his way of life. To the Jew who acts contrarily, the Torah is the guide to bring him back. In the final analysis, though, all Jews are HaShem's children and, in that reality and awareness, we may be comforted.

Parashas Eikev

Sefer Devarim witnesses the end of several longstanding relationships. The book, of course, constitutes Moshe's farewell speech to the people, but it also signals a change in the relationship between בני ישראל and HaShem. בני ישראל had enjoyed an intimate relationship with HaShem throughout their 40-year sojourn, sustained by Divine miracles on a daily basis. Their entrance into the Land of Israel, however, meant that the terms of that relationship had to change. Moshe's rhetoric in the opening section of the book, particularly in Parashas Eikev, seeks to facilitate a seamless transition to this new reality.

By setting down roots, spread throughout the land, בני ישראל would not have such direct access to the Divine. With HaShem not as obvious a presence in their daily lives, כיבוש הארץ threatened the viability of this fledgling nation. For those who had lived through the miracles of the מדבר, the desert, the transition to this new reality might cause them to forget the wonders that HaShem had performed on their behalf. Moshe's challenge in the book is to ensure that the generation that experienced unmediated access to the Divine is able to carry forward those experiences into their new existence in the Land. For this reason, Moshe reminds the people, at numerous points in the opening section of Sefer Devarim, of their experiences over the past 40 years. In this week's parasha, Moshe says, "Take care that you do not forget HaShem your God... When you have eaten your fill and have built fine houses and live in them... do not exalt yourself, forgetting HaShem your God" (Devarim 8:11-12, 14). Elaborating on this point, Moshe cautions the people, "not to say to yourself, 'My power and the might of my own hand have gotten me this wealth' " (Devarim 8:17). After all, says Moshe, HaShem had performed a plethora of miracles for the people, taking them out of Egypt, sustaining them in a barren wilderness with מן and with water that flowed out of rocks.

Moshe returns to the same theme later in the parasha, informing the people that the extensive miracles that they witnessed – yetzi'at mitzrayim, kri'at yam suf, the punishment of Datan and Aviram, and, more generally, "what He did for you in the wilderness before you arrived in this place" (Devarim 11:5) – impose a special obligation on that generation: "Remember today that your children were not the ones who saw and experienced the discipline of HaShem your God... But it was your own eyes that saw all these great things the Lord has done. Observe therefore all the commands I am giving you today" (Devarim 11:2, 7-8).

Moshe's challenge, however, is not only to ensure that his contemporaries take with them the memories of their experiences in the wilderness, but also to secure the commitment of future generations who never witnessed those miracles. In the passage above in chapter 11, immediately after reminding בני ישראל that they must not forget the miracles they witnessed, Moshe turns his attention to future generations, "Fix these words of mine in your hearts and minds; tie them as symbols on your hands and bind them on your foreheads. Teach them to your children, talking about them when you sit at home and when you walk along the road, when you lie down and when you get up. Write them on the doorframes of your houses and on your gates, so that your days and the days of your children may be many in the Land that HaShem swore to give your forefathers..." (Devarim 11:18-21). The current generation, it seems, has an obligation to transmit the knowledge that they acquired to their progeny, a generation that "were not the ones who saw and experienced the discipline of HaShem your God" (Devarim 11:2).

What lessons, exactly, does Moshe expect his contemporaries to teach their children? The commandment to "teach them to your children" (Devarim 11:19) is embedded within a passage that חז"ל took to refer to the mitzvot of tefillin and mezuzah. Moshe understood that future generations would not have access to the Divine revelation witnessed by his generation;

they would not hear HaShem's voice as had the דור המדבר. Their access to HaShem, then, would be via His mitzvos that were transmitted as part of that revelation. The generation that lived intimately with HaShem had a responsibility to pass on the lessons they learned through the commandments that they received.

Rashbam (Shemot 13:9) parted ways with most other Rishonim in his interpretation of what the Torah means by וקשרתם אתם לאות על ידכם והיו לטוטפת בין עיניכם, suggesting that, at least על פי פשט, this pasuk should be understood metaphorically: You should internalize God's will to such an extent that it is virtually emblazoned on your body. Ibn Ezra (Shemot 13:9) attributes a similar interpretation of וכתבתם על מזוזות ביתך ובשעריך to an unnamed contemporary. Of course, we take these psukim as referring to the performance of physical actions – tefillin and mezuzah – but the insight of Rashbam can enrich our appreciation of the contribution that mitzvos make to the ongoing vitality of the Jewish community. Mitzvos were not simply intended to be performed ritually; rather, they are the way in which we memorialize the word of God, Divine revelation, and HaShem's will for all time.

Moshe thus issues instructions to his contemporaries that will sustain not only them but also those who never lived through the miraculous events of the previous 40 years. Because the latter did not have the good fortune to witness Divine revelation, it is incumbent upon those who did to transmit the memory of those miracles through the medium of HaShem's mitzvos. When we perform mitzvos as vestiges of revelation and not simply as ritual acts, we too manage to connect with the miracles of the past.

Parashas Re'eh

Among the commandments in Parashas Re'eh is the prohibition against eating certain kinds of animals, birds and fish. The Torah explains in detail what is kosher and what may not be eaten. The dietary laws also include the separation of meat and dairy foods.

The section of the dietary laws is introduced by the following psukim, "For you are a holy people to HaShem, your G-d. And HaShem has chosen you for himself to be an עם סגולה, a treasured people from among all the peoples on the face of the earth" (Devarim 14:2-3). This paragraph concludes with a call to saintliness, כי עם קדוש אתה לה' אלקיך, "For you are a holy nation to HaShem, your G-d; you shall not cook a kid in its mother's milk" (Devarim 14:21).

The Rambam, in his *Guide to the Perplexed* (3:48), offers thought-provoking explanations for the dietary laws. He writes that the Torah forbids us to eat any food that is harmful and unhealthy. For instance, pork contains more moisture than is necessary. Furthermore, the pig is an animal with filthy eating habits, whose food is putrid and messy. The fat of its intestines produces constipation and has a negative effect on the blood circulation. The Rambam further suggests that man should eat vegetables, fruit and the meat of animals that the Torah permits. He concludes that all physicians would agree with his opinion.

The Ramban, a halachist, a great kabbalist, but also a physician by profession, shares the Rambam's rational approach on this subject, although he comes to his conclusions from a different stance. The Ramban goes on to explain that the criterion for forbidden birds, which are all birds of prey, is their clawing habits. In his commentary on Vayikra 11:13, he disqualifies them on account of their instinctive cruelty. According to the Ramban, birds of prey are forbidden for human consumption because their cruel nature can negatively influence the human being. As far as beasts are concerned, he declares that those animals that are identified by parted hoofs and that chew their cud are not ferocious and are therefore permitted for human consumption. The Ramban concurs with the Rambam on this issue.

In the 15th century, Abarbanel framed the subject of the dietary laws in an entirely different manner than either the Rambam or the Ramban. He espoused that the laws were given to safeguard not our bodies but our souls. Abarbanel wrote, "If I would believe what the Rambam and the Ramban wrote, then the Divine Torah would be nothing more than an abridged medical-dietary manual. Do we not see people eating pork and even mice, yet they are a model of health?" Then he continued, "The Torah does not legislate healthful prescriptions but rather cares for promoting the welfare of the soul." We read in Parashas Shemini, אל תשקצו את נפשתיכם, "You shall not make your soul detestable" (Vayikra 11:43), and Parashas Re'eh concludes, כי עם קדוש אתה, "For you are a holy nation to your G-d" (Devarim 14:2). It is the soul of the nation and the soul of the individual Jew that must be safeguarded.

However, we cannot continue without defending the Rambam. He wrote *The Guide to the Perplexed* from a philosophical point of view and dedicated the book to his student, Joseph ben Aknin, who was not well versed in the study of the Talmud. In addition, *The Guide to the Perplexed* is not a legal work that should be brought into a discussion of halachah. The magnum opus of the Rambam was the *Mishneh Torah*, 14 books that deal with all halachic decisions pertaining to Jewish life. The section that deals with kashrus is called by the Rambam "Sefer Kedushah," the book of sanctity. The word kedushah clearly conveys the views of the Rambam that the Torah commanded observance of kashrus to safeguard the sanctity of the Jewish soul. The Rambam concludes the section by noting that all who are meticulous in the observance of kashrus are sanctified by greater kedushah and purity of soul.

Since the student of the Rambam was not well versed in Talmudic studies, it was feared that he would not appreciate the statement of the rabbis in Yoma 39a, עבירה של אדם מטמטמת לבו, "the sin (of neglecting kashrus) dulls the heart of man," or the statement in Shabbos 145b that "the idolaters are lustful because they eat abominable creeping things." The Rambam felt it would be advantageous for the student to progress in his studies, after which he would teach him the laws of kashrus on a higher and more spiritual level. The Torah laws of kashrus are meant to protect the soul rather than the body of every Jewish person. Furthermore, the Rambam had already asserted the traditional point of view in the *Mishneh Torah* and wrote *The Guide to the Perplexed* two years before he passed away, for an audience of confused believers.

In summary, all these sages, without exception, believed that there may be reasons of health for kashrus observance, but the main purpose remains the safekeeping of the holiness of the Jewish soul.

Parashas Shoftim

The Sforno, in his 16th century commentary, introduces Parashas Shoftim with a short summary of its content. He states, "After having described the laws appertaining to the common citizen in the previous parshiyos, Moshe Rabbeinu now presents the laws concerning the leaders of the nation. They are the melech (king), shofet (judge), kohen (priest), and navi (prophet)." This essay discusses the rules and laws of the king, who represents the government of the Jewish people in ארץ ישראל.

The Torah reads, "When you come to the Land HaShem gives you... שום תשים עליך מלך, you shall surely set over yourself a king whom HaShem your G-d shall choose; מקרב אחיך תשים עליך מלך, from among your brethren shall you set a king over yourself" (Devarim 17:14-15).

The Gemara in Sanhedrin 20b discusses the question as to whether the appointment of a king is a חיוב or a רשות, i.e., mandatory or optional. The matter remains unresolved to this day. Rav Moshe Feinstein (1895-1986), the greatest halachist of our times, states that it is a חיוב (Igros Moshe). Before him, the Rambam quoted the Gemara in his opening halachah of Hilchos Melachim that three mitzvos were given to בני ישראל when they entered the Land: To appoint a king, to eradicate the seed of Amalek and to build the Beis Hamikdash. This halachah indicates that he considered the appointment of a king to be mandatory.

However, R Saadiah Gaon and many Rishonim, such as the Ramban (ad loc. Devarim 17:14) and Ibn Ezra (ad loc. Devarim 17:15), said that it is מותר, permitted, but not mandatory, to appoint a king. In the 15th century, Abarbanel wrote his commentary on Sefer Shmuel, in which there is a lengthy and extremely convincing exposition of his disagreement with the view that kingship is a חיוב. There, Shmuel HaNavi spells out all of the woes that will accrue to the nation that appoints a king (Shmuel I 8:11-18). Abarbanel concluded that the monarchy is a disaster, not only for the nations of the world but even more so for the Jewish people. He considered all kings to be corrupt despots.

Abarbanel further wrote that, in Parashas Re'eh, the Torah required that each Jewish king have a Sefer Torah written for himself and carry it with him at all times, in order that he fear HaShem, observe the Torah and avoid becoming haughty over his brethren. In spite of this precaution, in Abarbanel's opinion, most of the Jewish kings were not any better than the non-Jewish kings of whom he disapproved. Continuing his exposition, Abarbanel mentions that David, Chizkiyahu and Yoshiah were the only kings who were G-d-fearing. All of the other kings of Yehudah, and all of the kings of Yisrael – the kingdom of the ten tribes that seceded from Yehudah – were dedicated to idol worship. By contrast, all of the Shoftim who led Israel in the period following Yehoshuah's passing, but before the institution of the monarchy, were G-d-fearing men.

Looking at the Shoftim, Abarbanel deduced from this historical fact that the best government is not a monarchy but one elected by the people for a short period of time. He gave as an example the three Italian city-states of Florence, Venice and Genoa of the Middle Ages and early modern period, which flourished and survived for several centuries.

In the force of his argument, Abarbanel's critical view of the institution of monarchy remains unparalleled in rabbinic writings until today. Nonetheless, in our recent history, we find a great personality whose thoughts on the ideal self-government of the Jews are analogous to this position of Abarbanel. Rav Kook (1865-1935), the first chief rabbi of Israel, discusses the establishment of a Jewish government by democratic process in his book, *Mishpat Kohen*. In rendering a decision on this matter, Rav Kook wrote that when the Jewish nation would have the need to appoint a government, if there were no suitable candidate available from the House of David, and there was neither a prophet nor a Sanhedrin, then the

power to appoint a leader would revert, or rather return, to
כלל ישראל. The selection process would be similar to that
employed in the time of the Shoftim. The chosen shofet or
leader would have דין מלך, the judicial status of a king. But his
children would not have any claim to continue a dynasty and his
role would remain within the framework of a democratic
constitution.

In Rav Kook's writings, we find an opinion that echoes
Abarbanel's views on democracy. Rav Kook's statement,
although attracting controversy during his lifetime, insists that a
democratic process is both feasible and desirable. Surprisingly,
at the very beginning of the laws of Chanukah, the Rambam
declares that even though the kings of the Hashmonaim were
kohanim, contrary to halachah barring kohanim from becoming
kings, nevertheless HaShem helped them defeat the Greek
army. In addition, the Rambam explicitly describes the
Hasmonian rule as מלכות ישראל, the "Kingdom of Israel," which
lasted for 200 years until the destruction of the second Beis
Hamikdash (Hilchos Megillah veChanukah 3:1). Just as the
Rambam felt that the ascendancy of the Hashmonaim was
appropriate, it is clear that Rav Kook was also correct when he
stated, before the establishment of the State of Israel that it is
acceptable to appoint a government if there is no king, prophet,
or Sanhedrin. This has proved to be the politically and
halachically correct solution for our times.

In conclusion, since the time of the Shoftim there has been a
belief in government along democratic lines. These aspirations
may have now been realized and, every Shabbos, after we read
from the Torah, we pray for the State of Israel, which has a
government that gets its authority from כלל ישראל, as described
by Abarbanel, the Rambam and Rav Kook.

Parashas Ki Seitzei

When בני ישראל left Egypt (Devarim 25:17-19), the Torah states that Amalek attacked those Israelites who were at the rear and were faint and exhausted. The Torah emphasizes that Amalek לא ירא אלקים, did not fear HaShem. The Torah then concludes this section with an exhortation to בני ישראל: תמחה את זכר עמלק מתחת השמים, לא תשכח, "You shall wipe out the memory of Amalek from under the heaven, you shall not forget!" (Devarim 25:19).

Amalek has continued to hound בני ישראל throughout the ages, their unbridled hatred toward the Jewish people surfacing time and time again. For example, what did the Jews in Persia do that Haman sought their destruction? Such infinite enmity, even to the point of murderous destruction, stems from nothing but fanatical hatred without cause. Similarly, what did the Jews of Germany do to deserve their fate under the Nazis? They had lived in that region since the time of Charlemagne in the 10th century, well before the existence of the modern state of Germany. The goal of Amalek is to totally annihilate the Jewish nation, without reason. The Torah therefore says it is a mitzvah to wipe them out, to remember and never to forget.

The *Sefer Hachinuch* was written in the 14th or 15th century by an unknown author and explains all of the 613 mitzvos of the Torah as enumerated by the Rambam. In *Sefer Hachinuch*, special characteristics of the war against Amalek are explained. For example, prior to the war of conquest against the seven nations that inhabited Canaan, Yehoshua was first commanded to offer them the opportunity to accept the seven Noahide mitzvos or to emigrate to another land. Israel could wage war against them only if they refused these conditions. Women were allowed to participate in this war. Yet, in the war against Amalek, women were not allowed to participate. What, then, is the difference between the war against the seven nations and the war against Amalek?

The difference is that Amalek fights a war for the sake of killing Jews, i.e., a war for the sake of war. The Gemara explains that it is the way of men to make war, inferring that women are not warriors (Kiddushin 2b, Nazir 59a). Therefore, in a war fought merely for the sake of war – i.e., where there is no rationale for the war other than fighting itself – women, who are not warriors, cannot participate.

By contrast, in the war against the seven nations, those nations fought to defend the land they lived in. The Israelite men fought for the sake of כיבוש, taking possession of the Land, and ישוב הארץ, settling the Land. The mitzvah of settling the Land applies equally to women. Thus because of the rationale to wage the war against the seven nations, and because women were commanded to fight for ישוב הארץ, they were permitted to participate in the war.

In attempting to better understand the distinction between the war against the seven nations and the war against Amalek, we turn to the Rambam (Hilchos Melachim 5:4-5), who speaks at length about these two types of war. The Rambam says that it is a mitzvah to destroy the seven nations but concludes, with regard to this mitzvah, כבר אבד זכרם, that their memory has already been lost. In the next paragraph, the Rambam states that it is a mitzvah to destroy the memory of Amalek, to remember what they did to us and to never forget their hatred of the Jewish people. Tellingly, with regard to this war, he does not conclude with the words כבר אבד זכרם, implying that the war against Amalek continues today.

The Brisker Rav (1886-1959), the uncle of the late Rabbi J. B. Soleveitchik, was one of the greatest talmidei chachamim of his time. He explained that there is no memory today of the existence of the seven nations of ancient days because, as the Gemara (Berachot 28a) relates, כבר עלה סנחריב מלך אשור ובלבל את כל האומות, "Sennacharib king of Assyria long ago went up and mixed up all the nations." Sennacherib, the Assyrian king during the period of the first Beis Hamikdash, conquered mostof the ancient world and, in doing so, he intermingled most of the peoples of that time and place. Thus, even ancient Amalek exists no more.

However, the Brisker Rav teaches that although the physical remnant of Amalek may no longer exist, a person or a nation that has the total annihilation of the Jews as its goal is designated as Amalek. Acting like Amalek is being Amalek! By way of example, in the last century Nazi Germany acted with ruthless, murderous efficiency with the aim of the destruction of Jews worldwide and consequently embodied Amalek. Likewise, any state that today embraces radical Islam, calling for the destruction of Israel or killing Jews, becomes Amalek.

In conclusion, when Amalek came to attack בני ישראל on their way to ארץ ישראל, they knew that HaShem had brought Israel out of Egypt through extraordinary miracles. They knew that Israel is עם סגולה, HaShem's chosen nation. They knew that Israel represents HaShem in this world. Therefore, their attack on the Israelites was in fact a war against HaShem Himself. The Torah writes in Parashas Beshalach (Shemos 17:16), "I shall surely erase the name of Amalek from under the heavens" and "HaShem continues to maintain a war against Amalek from generation to generation." We, on the other hand, hope and pray for the end of war and that we will live to see the fulfillment of the words of Yeshayahu HaNavi, לא ישא גוי אל גוי חרב ולא ילמדו עוד מלחמה, "Nation will not lift sword against nation and they will no longer study warfare" (Yeshayahu 2:4). So fundamental are these prophetic words that they are inscribed publically on a wall across from the United Nations in New York.

Parashas Ki Savo

Parashas Ki Savo discusses the mitzvos of מקרא ביכורים, the "Declaration of Bikkurim," and וידוי מעשרות, the "Confession of the Tithes." The Torah begins by describing what will happen when the Children of Israel enter the Land of Israel and settle it, stating, "It will be when you enter the Land that HaShem your G-d gives it to you as an inheritance and you shall possess it and dwell in it" (Devarim 26:1). ארץ ישראל is renowned for the seven species it produces. The Torah prescribes that, as they ripen, בני ישראל must fulfill the mitzvah of bringing the bikkurim, the first fruits of the season, to the Beis Hamikdash in Yerushalayim. Chapter 3 of Mishnah Bikkurim offers a vivid, detailed description of this incredibly joyous occasion.

The bikkurim were brought from the various outlying districts to Yerushalayim by the farmers, accompanied by the מעמד, a group of representatives from the area charged with taking pilgrims to הר הבית, the Temple Mount. They would form a procession and make their way up to the Beis Hamikdash after the leader of the מעמד declared, קומו ונעלה ציון אל ה׳ אלוקינו, "Let us arise and go up to Zion, unto the House of HaShem," (Yirmiyahu 31:5). The farmer placed the basket containing the bikkurim on his shoulder and then recited a prayer before handing the basket to the Kohen. Because of the great importance of the prayer, the words had to be prescribed verbatim by the Torah. This is the only time that the Torah stipulates the words of a prayer and elevates the bringing of the bikkurim by the individual farmer to a national expression of love of HaShem and of the Land He has given to His people.

Over the centuries, חז״ל have offered many perushim on this parashah. Each word in the biblical mandate has its own unique and profound significance. With regard to the opening passage in the parashah (Devarim 26:1), when the Torah says "inherit," it means that the Nation of Israel has an indisputable and inalienable claim to all of the Land of Israel. "To dwell" tells us that בני ישראל belong to the Land and are at home there. The pasuk teaches that the Land was given as a national inheritance from our Patriarch, Avraham. As the Torah relates, HaShem told Avraham, לזרעך אתן את הארץ הזאת, "To your offspring I will give this Land" (Bereishis 12:7), i.e., that He would give the Land to Avraham's descendants, the People of Israel.

The Rambam, in his *Guide to the Perplexed* (39:3), offers additional insight into the mitzvah of bikkurim. He states that the first fruits were selected because all that is first in life is highly esteemed. Therefore that which is most honored and valued should be brought to the Beis Hamikdash as a gift of thanksgiving to HaShem, to whom we owe everything. When the farmer brings his bikkurim, he must also remember his days of hardship and struggle and the bitter bondage in Egypt, which stands for the ultimate national experience of hardship. The Rambam stresses that the farmer must learn to be humble before HaShem.

An illustration of this lesson in humility can be found in the aforementioned third chapter of Mishnah Bikkurim, where it states that King Agrippas I, the grandson of Herod, despite his worldliness and Hellenistic tendencies, observed the precepts of the Torah, including the mitzvah of bikkurim. The *Mishnah* (Bikkurim 3:4) relates that, when he came to the temple, he placed the basket of first fruits on his shoulder as a sign of humility.

There is a further significance to King Agrippas, who was not of pure Jewish descent, and his declaration of the bikkurim. Mishnah Sotah 7:8 tells us that when he read a passage in the Torah forbidding Israel to set a foreign king over them, he burst into tears. Consoling him, the sages said, אחינו אתה, "you are our brother." Therefore, when King Agrippas recited the words of the declaration of the bikkurim, כי באתי אל הארץ, "I came to this Land" (Devarim 26:3), he humbly wanted to share the destiny of the Jewish people.

Through the fulfillment of the mitzvah of bikkurim, we are shown that king and poor farmer alike can identify with the people of Israel because both share in the destiny of the Jewish nation that came from slavery in Egypt to the Land flowing with milk and honey. In fact, when Moshe makes the covenant of HaShem with Israel (in Parashas Nitzavim), the Torah clearly wishes us to identify with previous generations. At that time, Moshe declares, "Not with you alone do I seal this covenant and this oath, but with whoever is here, standing with us today before HaShem our G-d and with whoever is not here with us today" (Devarim 29:13-14). We see from this statement that the binding covenant remains a legacy for all future generations and this bond is affirmed in the declaration which accompanies the bringing of the bikkurim. This mitzvah will be fulfilled when the third Beis Hamikdash is rebuilt in the days of Mashiach, bimhera beyameinu.

Parashas Nitzavim-Vayeilech

The first 10 psukim in chapter 30 of Devarim form a unique section of Parashas Nitzavim. The theme of these psukim is the future repentance and redemption of Israel. In chapter 30, verse 2 we read, ושבת עד ה' אלקיך, "And you shall return unto HaShem your G-d and listen to His voice, according to everything that I command you today, you and your children, with all your heart and all your soul." This pasuk is speaking about the repentance of Israel. The next pasuk, verse 3, reads, ושב ה' אלקיך את שבותך ורחמך ושב וקבצך מכל העמים אשר חפיצך ה' אלקיך שמה, "HaShem your G-d will return your captivity and have compassion on you. He will return and gather you in from all the peoples to which HaShem your G-d has scattered you." This pasuk is referring to the return to ארץ ישראל, the Final Redemption.

The Rishonim agree that the central theme of this parashah is תשובה which, in verse 2, refers to our return to HaShem and, in verse 3, refers to HaShem restoring us to our homeland. However, they differ on the nature of the Final Redemption, whether Israel must always first repent to merit redemption, or whether the Jewish people can first be redeemed and afterwards do תשובה.

Before examining the words of the Rishonim, let us first look at the vision of Yechezkel who foresaw the return of the Jewish people in the End of Days, "Thus said HaShem, I will assemble you from the nations and gather you in from the lands where you have been scattered and give you the Land of Israel" (Yechezkel 11:17). Here, the prophet reveals that true repentance will begin in the Land. ונתתי להם לב אחד ורוח חדשה אתן בקרבכם, "I will give them an undivided heart, and I will place a new spirit in them" (11:19). The prophet Yechezkel is saying that קדושת ארץ ישראל, the holiness of ארץ ישראל, will enable the Jewish people to do full תשובה, with a new heart and a new spirit. Yechezkel prophesied that the redemption will come before repentance.

141

For our generation, the generation that experienced and participated in the process of ingathering of the exiles, there is great empathy for the revival and return of the Jewish people. We see a special message in what the Rambam writes at the very end of his 14-volume *Mishneh Torah*. There, in הלכות מלכים ומלחמותיהם, "the laws of Kings and their Wars" he states (11:1), "He who does not believe in the advent of Mashiach or is not looking forward to it, not only does he deny the words of the prophets, but even the words of the Torah and Moshe Rabbeinu as well." The Rambam then quotes the psukim of this parashah, ושב ה׳ אלקיך את שבותך ורחמך, "HaShem your G-d will turn back your captivity and have compassion upon you" (Devarim 30:3) and also the pasuk, אם יהיה נדחך בקצה השמים, "If your dispersed will be at the end of heaven..." (Devarim 30:4) and finally, והביאך ה׳ אלקיך אל הארץ אשר ירשו אבתיך, "HaShem will bring you to the Land that your forefathers possessed..." (Devarim 30:5). Here, the Rambam declares that Parashas Nitzavim is meant to teach the concept that גאולה, redemption, will come by the hand of HaShem before the repentance of all of Israel.

This view is supported by the Ramban, as mentioned by the Netziv (R. Tzvi Yehudah Berlin, d. 1893), who was the Rosh Yeshivah of the famous Volozhner Yeshivah. The Netziv quotes the Ramban, who states in his commentary on Shir Hashirim 8:12 that a small number of the Jewish people will return to ארץ ישראל and will live there forever with the consent and assistance of the nations (see Parashas Beha'aloscha). According to the Ramban, the people will return and, thereafter, תשובה will follow.

In the same period, the *Zohar*, the central work of Kabbalah, attributed to the Tanna Rabbi Shimon bar Yochai, foresees the return of the Jewish people to ארץ ישראל at the time when the sons of Yishmael will conspire together with all of the people of the world to take Yerushalayim. That is to say, we must return to the Land before some kind of perfect repentence; redemption precedes תשובה.

This generation is witnessing the beginning of the redemption. The establishment of the State of Israel is the greatest national aliyah ever. In *אורות התשובה*, *Lights of Repentance*, Rav Kook writes, "The glimmerings of תשובה exist in Israel. The arousing of the will of the nation as a whole to return to its homeland, to its own essence... contains something of the genuine light of repentance." The majority of Jews now live in ארץ ישראל. We should follow the עניין that רובה ככולה, a majority is like the totality.

In conclusion, when a majority of the Jewish people decide to return as a nation to their homeland, they do תשובה collectively and usher in the גאולה as described in this parashah, chapter 30 verses 2 and 3. This period in which we live is אתחלתא דגאולה; it is in this return to the Land of Israel that תשובה and גאולה take place together.

Parashas Ha'azinu

Parashas Ha'azinu is the shortest parashah, with 52 psukim of chapter 32 in Sefer Devarim. Its first 43 psukim are designated as שירת משה, the Song of Moshe. It recounts the story of בני ישראל from its birth as a nation until the end of time. While the word שירה is most often translated as "song," the English word song refers to something lighter; שירת משה is Divine prophecy expressed in poetic form.

In his commentary on Ha'azinu, the Ramban gives one of his most in-depth analyses in the Torah and his expansive vision for this parashah is unique among all of the commentators. The Ramban declares that the שירה speaks of the past, present and future of of בני ישראל. In so doing, it tells of the historic relationship between HaShem and the Jewish people, and how HaShem reciprocated the behavior of His nation.

First, the שירה describes HaShem's Divine loving-kindness from the time He elected Israel as his chosen nation. Next, it tells of His benevolence, His protection and His care of Israel during its long trek through the מדבר. Finally, it recounts the Divine support of the nation in its conquest of the Holy Land.

From that point, according to the Ramban, the שירה goes on to depict Israel living in prosperity and plenty in its Land. Yet out of opulence and wellbeing sprang forth rebellion. Israel deserted HaShem for idolatry. The שירה then proceeds to describe Divine misgivings resulting from Israel's betrayal and the punitive measures that descended upon them: First famine, then pestilence and massacres, followed by expulsion, at which point Israel would be scattered to the four corners of the world. History has confirmed the truth of this prophecy as all of this has come to pass.

Nevertheless, in the midst of the darker parts of the prophecy, the verse states, אשיב נקם לצרי ולמשנאי אשלם, "I [HaShem] will return vengeance upon My enemies, and upon they that hate Me I shall bring retribution" (Devarim 32:41). The Ramban explains this passage to mean that HaShem declares that the enemies of His people are His enemies. History has shown that those nations that harmed the Jewish people were always avenged by HaShem.

The Ramban further comments that the שירה is not a series of rebukes against Israel. Furthermore, it offers no conditions on returning to HaShem and worshipping Him in truth and out of love. It is significant, according to the Ramban, that the parashah does not mention that Israel must do תשובה. Unlike Parashas Nitzavim, where the interplay between תשובה and גאולה is described, this parashah is a historical testimony, bearing witness to the suffering that Israel would endure when its people did not live according to the Torah.

The promise of the שירה is that, even if Israel perpetuates its sins against HaShem and is punished, the nation will never cease to exist.

Despite the frightening statements of the prophecy, the שירה ends on a happy note:

הרנינו גוים עמו כי דם עבדיו יקום ונקם ישיב לצריו וכפר אדמתו עמו

"O nations, sing the praise of His people!

For He will avenge the blood of His servants,

He will bring retribution upon His foes,

And He will appease His Land and His people" (Devarim 32:43).

The Ramban comments that שירת משה is clearly intended to apply to אחרית הימים, the Final Redemption at the end of time. He states that the prophecy does not apply to the return of the exiles from Bavel because, at that time, the nations did not sing the praises of those who returned, as stated in the pasuk above, "O nations, sing the praise of His people!" On the contrary, the exiles from Bavel were met only with derision, as we read in Nehemyah 3:34: מה היהודים האמללים עשים, "What are those Jewish weaklings doing?" Therefore, the prophecy will occur at the end of time, when the Jewish people return to the Land of Israel and the Final Redemption takes place. At that time,

HaShem will avenge the blood of His servants and He will "appease the land and His people."

In Yeshayahu, HaShem proclaims with regard to the time of the final redemption, בעתה אחישנה אני ה׳, "I am HaShem; in its time, I will hasten it" (Yeshayahu 60:22). There is a famous debate in the Gemara regarding this prophecy. Rabbi Eliezer strongly believed that Israel would be redeemed only through repentance. Arguing against him, Rabbi Yehoshua exclaimed that Israel would hasten redemption if it repents, as the pasuk states, but that even if it does not repent, redemption will eventually come, בעתה אחישנה, at its Divinely appointed time. Their debate goes back and forth until Rabbi Eliezer finally remains silent, signifying that he concedes and that repentance is not a precondition for redemption (Sanhedrin 98a; see Hatekufah Hagedolah, chapter 6).

The Ramban accepted the silence of Rabbi Eliezer as the Gemara's final decision, that at the end of time, in the days of גאולה, the Jewish people will be redeemed, even without the merit of complete תשובה and will have, as Yechezkel HaNavi states, לב חדש ורוח חדשה, a "new heart and a new spirit" (Yechezkel 36:26). For the Ramban, this is the future envisioned by the Divine prophecy in poetic form of שירת משה. When we consider that Jews have returned to ארץ ישראל from the four corners of the world, we are encouraged to believe that this prophecy is finally coming to pass and that we are living in the period of אתחלתא דגאולה.

Parashas Vezos Haberachah

The last parashah of the Torah, Vezos Haberachah in Sefer Devarim, chapters 33 and 34, contains Moshe's parting blessing to the people of Israel, and the description of Moshe's final dialogue with HaShem before his death and burial.

The parashah narrates Moshe's blessings to בני ישראל. It is interesting to note some similarities and differences between the benedictions of Moshe in this parashah and those of Yaakov Avinu in Parashas Vayechi (Bereishis, chapters 49-50). In general, Yaakov addresses his children as individuals whereas Moshe bestows his blessings on a nation encamped before him by tribe, awaiting entry to the Promised Land. Notice also that Moshe's blessings are formulated more as prayers for the success of the tribes whilst those of Yaakov are more individual, evaluating the personalities of his sons and their actions, and according them merit or demerit based on their behavior. Yaakov is addressing בני יעקב, his biological children, while Moshe is addressing בני ישראל, the children of Israel as a nation.

Ibn Ezra points out a comparison and a contrast between the two sets of berachos: Moshe does not mention the tribe of Shimon in his blessings. Yaakov mentions Shimon and Levi (Bereishis 49:5-7), but castigates them for their violent and reckless behavior toward the inhabitants of Shechem (Bereishis 34:30). Yet Moshe does bless the tribe of Levi. Why? Because Aharon merits a blessing that the entire tribe of Levi shares in the benediction of Aharon, while the tribe of Shimon did not produce such a meritorious personality.

According to the Ramban, the Torah wants to present no more than 12 tribes: כל אלה שבטי ישראל שנים עשר, "All these are the 12 tribes of Israel" (Bereishis 49:28).

Yaakov includes all of his 12 sons. In this parashah, however, Shimon is excluded, seemingly bringing the count down to a total of 11. Therefore, Yosef is represented by his two sons, Ephraim and Menashe, brigning the count back up to 12. Moshe already saw fit to mention Yosef as two tribes, saying about Yosef, והם רבבות אפרים והם אלפי מנשה, "and they are ten thousands of Ephraim and they are the thousands of Menashe" (Devarim 33:17). This, in turn, arose from the fact that HaShem had already designated them in that way by representing the two tribes as Yosef at the inauguration of the משכן (Bamidbar 7:48). All the tribes brought an offering and, rather than Yosef, it is Ephraim and Menashe that do so.

Sforno shed light on these blessings with an observation, which is also useful in defining the difference between the blessings of Moshe and those of Yaakov. He observes that Moshe addresses HaShem in his blessings, speaks of the tribes in the third person and also prays to HaShem for them. Yaakov's benedictions are directed in the second person, directly to his children. In that way, Yaakov blesses while Moshe prays. What distinguishes prayers from blessings? Prayer is addressed to HaShem whereas a blessing is conferred upon a person for deserving behavior. That said, Moshe does bless the people in this parashah, turning to behold them for the last time,וזאת הברכה אשר ברך משה, "and this is the blessing with which Moshe blessed [Bnei Yisrael]" (Devarim 33:1).

As this is the last parashah, it contains the death of Moshe Rabenu. וימת שם משה עבד ה׳, "Moshe, the servant of HaShem, died there" (Devarim 34:5). There is a famous question, if Moshe was writing down the Torah and the pasuk says he dies, how was the end of the Torah written? Rashi quotes the Gemara in giving two possible answers. The first is that Moshe wrote the Torah up to that point, and Yehoshua wrote the remaining psukim. The other is that HaShem dictated these words to Moshe, who wrote them with tears (Bava Basra 15b).

According to Abarbanel, Rabbenu Bachya, Ibn Ezra and many other mefarshim, HaShem in fact commanded Moshe to die and Moshe thereby fulfilled a מצות עשה, a positive commandment, with his death. Abarbanel goes further, saying that because the Torah says that Moshe died על פי ה׳, "by the mouth of HaShem," or as Rashi explains, "with HaShem's kiss," he did not die a normal death; he passed away immediately, without any pain, with total attachment to the Highest Source.

In the opening verse of the parashah, Moshe is given a title that has not previously been given to him in the Torah, משה איש האלקים, "Moshe, the man of G-d." Some commentators see this title as an emphasis on his prophetic power and an indication of his Divine authority. As the Torah says, ולא קם נביא עוד בישראל כמשה, "there arose no prophet in Israel as Moshe who spoke with HaShem face to face" (Devarim 34:10).

The seventh of the Rambam's Thirteen Principles of Faith reads, אני מאמין באמונה שלמה שנבואת משה רבנו עליו השלום היתה אמיתית ושהוא היה אב לנביאים לקודמים לפניו ולבאים אחריו", I believe with perfect faith that the prophecy of Moshe Rabbeinu, peace be upon him, was true, and that he was the chief of the prophets, both those that preceded and those that followed him." In this way, Rambam reminds the Jewish people in his day and in our days to honor the legacy of Moshe Rabbeinu and to live by HaShem's Torah and mitzvos.

26389418R00087

Made in the USA
Lexington, KY
06 October 2013